ALSO BY YIYUN LI

Wednesday's Child
The Book of Goose
*Tolstoy Together: 85 Days of War and Peace with
    Yiyun Li*
Must I Go
Where Reasons End
*Dear Friend, from My Life I Write to You in
    Your Life*
The Story of Gilgamesh
Kinder Than Solitude
Gold Boy, Emerald Girl
The Vagrants
A Thousand Years of Good Prayers

THINGS IN NATURE MERELY GROW

THINGS
IN
NATURE
MERELY
GROW

Yiyun Li

 FARRAR, STRAUS AND GIROUX   NEW YORK

Farrar, Straus and Giroux
120 Broadway, New York 10271

Printed in the United States of America
First edition, 2025

The extract on pages 85–86 is from "If Not Now, Later," by Yiyun Li,
The New Yorker, October 30, 2023.

Library of Congress Cataloging-in-Publication Data
Names: Li, Yiyun, 1972– author.
Title: Things in nature merely grow / Yiyun Li.
Description: First edition. | New York : Farrar, Straus and Giroux, 2025.
Identifiers: LCCN 2024057117 | ISBN 9780374617318 (hardcover)
Subjects: LCSH: Li, Yiyun, 1972-—Family. | Bereavement. |
    LCGFT: Creative nonfiction.
Classification: LCC PS3612.I16 T45 2025 | DDC 813/.6 [B]—
    dc23/eng/20250101
LC record available at https://lccn.loc.gov/2024057117

Designed by Abby Kagan

Our books may be purchased in bulk for promotional, educational,
or business use. Please contact your local bookseller or the Macmillan
Corporate and Premium Sales Department at 1-800-221-7945, extension
5442, or by email at MacmillanSpecialMarkets@macmillan.com.

www.fsgbooks.com
Follow us on social media at @fsgbooks

10   9   8   7   6   5   4   3   2   1

For Dapeng

And in memory of Vincent and James,
brothers and best friends

I was the world in which I walked, and what I saw
Or heard or felt came not but from myself;
And there I found myself more truly and more
    strange.

—WALLACE STEVENS, "Tea at the Palaz of Hoon"

THINGS IN NATURE MERELY GROW

I

There Is No Good Way to Say This

There is no good way to say this—when the police arrive, they inevitably preface the bad news with that sentence, as though their presence had not been ominous enough. The first time I heard the line, I knew already what was about to be conveyed. Nevertheless, I paid attention to how the news was delivered: the detective insisted that I take a seat first. I sat down at the dinner table, and he moved another chair to the right distance and sat down himself. No doubt he was following protocol, and yet the sentence—there is no good way to say this—struck me as both accurate and effective. It must be a sentence that, though nearly a cliché, is not often used in daily conversation; its precision has stayed with me.

The second time, having guessed the news about to be delivered, I did not give the sentence a moment's thought. I did not wait for the detective to ask me to sit down, either. I indicated a chair where my husband should sit and took the other chair in the living room. My heart already began to feel that sensation for which there is no name. Call it aching, call it wrenching, call it shattering, but they are all wrong words, useless in their familiarity. This time, the four policemen all stood.

There is no good way to state these facts, which must be acknowledged before I go on with this book. My husband and I had two children and lost them both: Vincent in 2017, at sixteen, James in 2024, at nineteen. Both chose suicide, and both died not far from home; James near Princeton Station, Vincent near Princeton Junction.

The detectives in charge of the two cases belonged to two agencies—one associated with Amtrak and the other with New Jersey Transit. As I type these facts, I come to a sudden realization, which was not available to me a few months earlier, or even yesterday. The facts would explain the confusion of the New Jersey Transit detective when he told me, on his second visit, that he couldn't locate Vincent's record in the files. He had an uneasy demeanor, perhaps feeling defeated by his inability to find Vincent or feeling the discomfort of having to face us again. On his first visit, he did all he could to avoid any reference to suicide, repeating the words "we can't say more at the moment" and "active investigation" and "the crime scene." Despite his fumbling, I already knew that James had died from suicide. I was the one to tell him that James's brother had died of suicide near Princeton Junction a little over six years ago.

My friend Elizabeth, who had arrived from Austin, Texas, just in time to be with us before the detective's scheduled visit, shook her head afterward. "Not quite competent, is he?" she said, and I agreed. I then told her about the other detective, who, on his second visit, had told us that he had worked for Amtrak for over twenty years, and every time he visited a family left by suicide, he would go home and hug his two children, even after they had outgrown the age to be hugged. It's an awkward truth that I cannot help observing and noticing things even in the most terrible moments.

It was the seventh day after James's death, and the New Jersey Transit detective was visiting a second time to return James's backpack, just as the Amtrak detective had come back to return Vincent's phone. A case involving life and death never miraculously closes itself at the time of the pronounced death.

Objects don't die. Their journeys in this physical world,

up to a certain point, are parallel to the trajectories of the humans to whom the objects belong. Then comes the moment when the separation happens. Vincent's phone became a phone, James's backpack, a backpack. They became objective objects, left behind in strangers' hands.

Few objects speak. The phone and the backpack were reticent, so they could do little to illuminate the last moments of my children's lives.

Many objects outlive people—this thought has often occurred to me when I see in a museum an eighteenth-century pianoforte or a twelfth-century sword or a bowl from 500 BCE. All of Vincent's belongings and all of James's belongings have outlived them; not a single item has left our care. There are Vincent's many paintings hung around the house. There is James's collection of pocket watches on a shelf. Everywhere I turn in the house there are objects: their meanings reside in the memories connected to them; the memories limn the voids, which cannot be filled by the objects.

Vincent's copy of *Les Misérables*, with a bust of Victor Hugo placed on top of it; a circle of blue and white farm animals from Delft next to a cluster of origami animals James had folded; a giant stuffed lamb bought on a drive through west Ireland, which James named Marmalade and called his emotional support animal during a prolonged trip (he often felt anxious when he had to leave home); a doorstop in the shape of a quietly amused elephant, bought in Kilkenny, which has been sitting next to James's computer for years; another doorstop, an owl with a startled expression, which Vincent picked up in an Edinburgh shop for James; forty-seven stuffed penguins of all shapes and colors, from different cities and countries, sitting in the middle of which is a crystal penguin brought by Vincent's childhood friend to his memorial service.

> To think our former state a happy dream:
> From which awaked, the truth of what we are
> Shows us but this: I am sworn brother, sweet,
> To grim necessity.

Sometimes, walking around the house, among the objects I study closely or only glance at, I recite Richard II's woeful words to myself. And yet I am not that dethroned king, our house is not a museum or a shrine, and our past is not merely a happy dream. I am not awakened, as I have stayed awake; I have been attentive and alert throughout all those years as the mother of my children. The necessity I face has no need of that adjective, "grim." Necessity—my necessity—is an extremity: any adjective is an irrelevance when it comes to extremity.

When the New Jersey Transit detective expressed his surprise at not being able to find Vincent's record, I only nodded as though to say such things were expected: life is a muddle, bureaucratically, factually, metaphorically. I was eager for him to leave so my husband and I could have the backpack to ourselves.

But sometimes—just sometimes—things make a little more sense upon revisiting. I wouldn't have solved that small mystery about the police agencies had I not started this book for James. "The book for James"—for months I have been talking about it with my friends Brigid and Elizabeth, calling it "the book for James," just as once I was writing "the book for Vincent."

Inevitably there comes that moment when *the* book—which takes up one's time, energy, mental space, even life—becomes *a* book. And then it's no more than an object, bearing a title, going on its own journey, parting ways with its author. This has happened to every book I've written, including the one for Vincent.

That earlier book—"the book for Vincent"—arrived without any conscious planning. One night, I was reading an Ivy Compton-Burnett novel, in which a character addresses her mother as "Mother dear." Mother dear—a phrase sounding archaic and yet ever lively and present—Vincent used to jokingly call me that when he wanted my attention. So the book arrived, opening with that phrase.

Vincent died at the end of September; by the end of November, I knew the book was finished. This time, I was conscious that I hadn't written a single word for James in that time frame. I kept telling Brigid that I knew the book was there; only, I couldn't find a way to write it.

Those who knew Vincent all knew that he would have loved the book for Vincent. He would have been proud and amused; he would have found fault with some of the sentences; he would have added a few adjectives and adverbs where I'd insisted on keeping sentences unadorned. The book, in which a mother and a dead child continue their conversation across the border of life and death, was as much written *for* Vincent as it was written *by* Vincent.

But in life James resisted metaphor and evaded attention. If Bartleby and Hamlet could merge into a singular being, James might have occupied that space with some comfort. ("'Seems,' madam? Nay, it is; I know not 'seems'" and "I would prefer not to.")

Brigid, quoting the opening line of a novel I had written some years ago—"Posterity, take notice!"—explained my difficulty to myself. A mother writes a book after her child's death, and that book could become a child's request for attention. James, Brigid said, is the antithesis of attention. It would be nearly impossible to write *for* James, she said; it feels as though you have to learn a new alphabet before you can write anything this time.

Learning a new alphabet—for weeks and months I've held on to that notion. James was a different child than

Vincent, and James's death left us in a different place than Vincent's death. And yet a new alphabet can only be symbolic, as I have but this old language to work with. Words tend to take on a flabbiness or a staleness after a catastrophe, but if one has to live with the extremity of losing two children, an imperfect and ineffective language is but a minor misfortune.

There is no good way to say this: words fall short.

And yet these two clichés speak an irrefutable truth. Anything I write for James is bound to be a partial failure. Sooner or later there will come the moment when my understanding parts ways with his essence. I can ask questions—answerable or unanswerable—but it is likely that by the end of the book I will have failed to find the right questions, just as I will have failed to pinpoint the exact moment when James's contemplation of suicide shifted from Vincent's to his own.

II

A Matter of Facts

There is no good way to say this. Facts are the harshest and the hardest part of life, and yet facts, unalterable, bring with them some order and logic.

Fiction, I've learned from writing it and reading it, tends to be about the inexplicable and the illogical. Sometimes my students complain about what they read in fiction—I don't believe this would happen in life, or, I don't believe any parent would do that to their children. What can I say to a young person who has strong convictions but a failure of the imagination? Not much, really. The world, it seems to me, is governed by strong conviction and paltry imagination and meager understanding.

In eighth grade, Vincent quoted C. S. Lewis in his application for a highly selective prep school in California—"I fancy that most of those who think at all have done a great deal of their thinking in the first fourteen years"—and went on to catalog the thinking he had done. Sometimes I give the Lewis quote to my undergraduates, and more than half of them—after having made it all the way to an elite university—express disbelief. When are you going to start thinking?—I try very hard not to ask the students, whose faces are cloudlessly young. They must be extraordinarily fortunate and extraordinarily clueless if they cannot believe it possible for them or for others to have done a great deal of thinking in the first fourteen years of their lives.

I have no doubt Vincent and James both did their share of thinking, which will remain a solace for me. And yet, one can always point out the opposite. No one commits suicide unthinkingly.

A few weeks before Vincent's death, we decided to purchase a house we all liked (we had just relocated that summer to Princeton). Vincent pointed out what would be his "suite"—a spacious bedroom, a bathroom, and a small study with a dormer window overlooking a tree, which looked nondescript in the fall, but would be blooming when spring came again: a dogwood tree.

The suite could be separated by a door from "the

parents' living quarters," Vincent pointed out, a perfect setting for him. He also envisioned baking in the kitchen and helping me improve the garden, which did not look too impressive: the couple who'd occupied the house before us, both economists, were not keen gardeners.

Vincent died on the day we put down the deposit for the house. Deposit, death, in that order, four hours apart. I would never have put those two things on the same day in a novel. In writing fiction, one avoids coincidences like that, which offer convenient metaphor, shoddy poignancy, and unearned drama. Life, however, does not follow a novelist's discipline. Fiction, one suspects, is tamer than life.

Some fiction is tamer than some life, I should amend. And I confess that this is only a variation of a statement made by Clare Aubrey, one of my favorite characters in Rebecca West's Saga of the Century trilogy. Clare, upon discovering her husband's extramarital affair, rereads *Madame Bovary* and exclaims, "But art is so much more real than life. Some art is much more real than some life, I mean."

In this life of mine, which makes some fiction feel pale and feeble, there are other facts that I need to establish before going on with this book.

Vincent and James were born three years, four months, and six days apart. The gap between their deaths: six years, four months, and nineteen days. These numbers and dates are carved into my mind more deeply than they could be into stone, but they convey very little.

To travel from Princeton to New York we have the choice of departing from either Princeton Station or Princeton Junction. This is an astonishing fact, though minor in the scale of things. I don't think I've developed a preference between the two. I leave from one station or the other, depending on my schedule and also on how finicky the train service is on that day. My husband has a more consistent way of dealing with this small problem. So at least in one specific aspect of life, he has certainty.

My feeling, not only about the departing stations but about almost everything in my life, is something else altogether. Call it a combination of keen attention and "a profound indifference" (borrowing Camus's words), or a combination of intense emotion and an equally intense apathy. The fact is, there is no word for this state I've found myself in, in which lucidity and opacity are one and the same.

The day after James's death, I said to Brigid, "One has to muddle through this life."

That statement was not accurate. There was something stark and piercing in me, which was much closer to clarity than to muddle, but calling it a muddle took less effort. It was as though I were averting my eyes from a mirror, which reflected my mind to me in such an unrelenting and sharp manner that I was startled by myself, frightened, even. By looking away one could imagine a muddled image, vaguer, softer, and less unsettling.

"But you're not muddled," Brigid said. For over twenty years she's been the first reader of my writing, and she never lets a wrong word or a weak sentence slip past. "You're the least muddled person at this moment."

True, my mind was not—and is not—muddled. Only, language is limited. So here's Exhibit A: a new alphabet and a new vocabulary cannot be found to describe how I feel.

Though I wouldn't call myself a sworn sibling to grim necessity, nevertheless necessity has been in everything I do since James's death. Gone are the days when I could afford some degree of automatic living in everyday life: shoes slipped on thoughtlessly (the pair of sneakers that used to be next to my shoes are in a different place now), a local detour taken without conscious thought (this road would lead to the corner where I last said goodbye to James), a quick stop at the university cafeteria (where my colleague and friend Ed and I both hid our faces when James, who was a freshman at Princeton, walked past us; he didn't notice us).

Necessity dictates that attention should be given to all details in this after-time: everything is relevant, everything has weight, and everything leads to a moment in the past, which becomes a memory, which in turn becomes a narrative. When a line of coral-colored hyacinths called Gipsy Queen bloomed next to the garden fence in March, I reminded myself, every time I walked past, to slow down and study them. James was the one to have loved this specific hyacinth; I used to prefer Delft Blue.

Necessity also dictates that all the details should be noticed and filed away without any excessive feeling.

After Vincent died, I read and reread *Grief Lessons*, a collection of Euripides's plays translated by Anne Carson, and Constance's monologue in Shakespeare's *King John*, after she lost young Arthur, who had been robbed of his throne and then his life. Those ancient Greeks sing their grief at the highest pitch, which, as Carson pointed out, is rage. Their grief and their rage are nearly untranslatable, as though feelings in extremity can only be physical sensations—the language assails the readers with a blind and blunt force. Constance, when chastised by Cardinal Randolph for her lack of composure ("Lady, you utter madness and not sorrow"), retorts:

> I am not mad: this hair I tear is mine;
> My name is Constance: I was Geoffrey's wife:
> Young Arthur is my son, and he is lost.
> I am not mad; I would to heaven I were,
> For then, 'tis like I should forget myself.

Oh, if I could, what grief should I forget!
Preach some philosophy to make me mad,
And thou shalt be canonized, cardinal.
For, being not mad but sensible of grief,
My reasonable part produces reason
How I may be delivered of these woes,
And teaches me to kill or hang myself.
If I were mad, I should forget my son,
Or madly think a babe of clouts were he.
I am not mad. Too well, too well I feel
The different plague of each calamity.

The ancient Greeks and Constance might have said something I could not find words for after Vincent died, and yet this statement is not entirely accurate. Those mothers in the Greek and Shakespearean tragedies voiced their sorrows at a higher pitch than mine. I did not lose my words and I was not at a loss for words when Vincent died. I wrote a book for him.

I also, on one occasion, wept. A few weeks after Vincent's death, Brigid and I went to see a production of *King Lear* in New York. By the time Lear finished his howling monologue, I was weeping; I went on weeping when we left the theater, sitting on the edge of a stone planter, in the center of which a small tree was shedding its last leaves. When I stopped crying, I said to Brigid, "There's no surprise left for me. No one will ever be able to surprise me after Vincent."

How one misspeaks, and how one misspeaks in extremity. James surprised me more than Vincent did, but this time, I know not to make any statement of finality.

This time, rereading Euripides and Shakespeare, I have a different reaction: make Constance's words a hundred times shriller, make those Greek mothers' cries a hundred times more piercing, and I would say, this is close to how I could express myself, too; only, I would prefer not to.

The truth is that however I choose to express myself will not live up to the weight of these facts: Vincent died, and then James died; through writing, I was able to conjure up a Vincent in the book written for him, but I will not be able to do this for James—I cannot conjure him up in any manner.

When Vincent was alive, we talked and we argued (sometimes affectionately and sometimes contentiously). It was only natural that our endless talking in life would extend itself to where reasons end, where across the border of life and death words retain their vivacity. The book for Vincent was published as fiction because it could only be called that: no dead child has ever come back to have an argument with his mother.

Two years after Vincent died, his friend Joy visited us

and told me she had read the book. "It's so uncanny," she said. "All those things he said in the book were just the things he would've said. When I was reading it, I thought, Vincent is back!" She laughed and then broke into tears.

Vincent had many good friends, and many, when he died, said things along the lines that they would always remember him. Joy, however, uncannily prescient at sixteen, expressed her fear that as years went by, she would not be able to remember Vincent as clearly as she wanted.

At least I'd given Joy a book to go by, I thought then.

I once edited out a few adjectives from Vincent's writing when he was in sixth grade, which led him to protest: "Adjectives and adverbs are my guilty pleasure!"

Well, then, words are my guilty pleasure. And my joy, too. And the only way I can make some sense out of this senseless life. Words are what I will do for James, too, even if I cannot learn a new alphabet and invent a new language, even knowing, right before starting, the inevitability of failing him.

James loved languages, though he was not a verbal child. He had been uncharacteristically talkative with Vincent, but with the rest of the world he had preferred silence. That silence became more pronounced after Vincent died.

The summer before James went to college, he confessed that he had done little in his senior year of high school but read five major works of Wittgenstein. I started to read *Tractatus Logico-Philosophicus*, on James's recommendation. A few weeks later, I told him that I had difficulty grasping what I was reading.

Oh, he replied with a single word, which could mean, not surprising, or, how could you not understand Wittgenstein, or, I don't know what I can do to help you, or, simply, read on.

This morning, I reread the introduction to *Tractatus Logico-Philosophicus*, which opens with this paragraph: "This book will perhaps only be understood by those who have themselves already thought the thoughts which are expressed in it—or similar thoughts. It is therefore not a text-book. Its object would be attained if there were one person who read it with understanding and to whom it afforded pleasure."

It's a solace to know that James found philosophical pleasure in language, different from the pleasure Vincent had got from language, which was poetic, musical, and sensual.

It's an impossible task to write a book for James. It will have to be done through thinking, rather than feeling; that is how I will reach for an approximation of understanding James. Or of not understanding him—just as I might spend my days reading Wittgenstein, not knowing if I've got anything right.

III

Found in an Abyss

(And a Disclaimer for Those Who Are Not the Right Readers)

A few weeks after James died, I wrote to Jane, a colleague who works in theater: "Our life seems to have entered the realm of Shakespearean dramas or Greek tragedies." And she replied: "Your losses are indeed epic and unfathomably hard; no language of mine can meet that."

And yet life is still to be lived, inside tragedies, outside tragedies, and despite tragedies. Writing this book is a way to separate myself from that strange realm while simultaneously settling myself permanently into that realm.

One can write about facts feelingly, one can write about feelings matter-of-factly, but one should never evade facts. So here I am, in a dire place, which few parents live in (at least in a contemporary setting, where life is not ravished by man-made or natural disasters). I've decided to write this book starting with a single established fact: I am in an abyss.

We—my husband and I—are in an abyss. But I shall keep his part to a minimum in this book. He is the only other person who has experienced these losses; losses for which people use the adjectives "unimaginable" or "unfathomable" to describe them. But my husband is a private person, and I believe in Marianne Moore's words: "The deepest feeling always shows itself in silence; / not in silence, but restraint."

So, here's the fact: I am in an abyss. I did not stray into the abyss. I did not fall into the abyss. I was not bullied or persecuted by others and thrown into the abyss. Rather, inexplicably and stunningly, I simply am in an abyss.

I am not lost. The feeling of being lost—a disorientation akin to despair—occurred briefly after Vincent died. I remember, after dropping off James at school, driving under a leaden sky, thinking that there was nowhere for us to go.

But that thought of having nowhere to go, just as the statement that no one would surprise me after Vincent died, was an expression of hyperbole, which is unavoidable in anguish: feelings, unexamined, present themselves as thoughts; even, facts.

This time I have been careful not to mistake feelings as thoughts or facts. My feelings: stunned, but not lost. My thought: I am found in an abyss.

Some people (especially in China) make a fuss about my using the word "die" when I talk about the deaths in my life, equating this linguistic decision to coldheartedness or evil.

Indeed there are euphemisms one could use. The word "euphemism," coming from Greek *euphēmismós* and meaning the substitution of an auspicious word for an inauspicious one, may imply sensitivity, but it may also imply cowardice. It is the latter, rather than the former, that puts people in the mood to censor and demonize.

Death, particularly suicide, cannot be softened or sugarcoated. After Vincent died, a couple of mothers asked me if they could tell their children—Vincent's peers—that he had died in an accident. That they preferred to lie to their children, even though the truth would surely reach those children through their friends, baffled me. I explained to the mothers that their proposal seemed to me a disrespect of their own children and a violation of Vincent's memory. Not calling a fact by its name can be the beginning of cruelty and injustice.

A few days after James's death, I told my friend Elizabeth, half-jokingly, that I would write a self-help book about radical acceptance. Radical acceptance was what sustained me then. The questions of whys and hows and wherefores or the wishful thinking of what-ifs: these questions naturally arise after any catastrophe, as they did after Vincent's death. But this time it feels to me that those questions, which function as a series of counterarguments against a fact, are useless; even, a violation of James's essence.

Those questions easily slip into the realm of alternatives. In writing fiction, one works with alternatives. "What E. M. Forster has called the 'flat' character has no alternatives at all"—Elizabeth Bowen said in her essay on novel writing. But in life, death does not come with an alternative.

My only grasp of the situation—then as well as now—is to accept that James, like Vincent, chose death, and James, particularly, chose the same way to die as Vincent. Reality, which can be conveyed in many ways, is better spoken of in the most straightforward language.

Elizabeth listened to my proposed self-help book and replied that most people would throw it across the room before finishing page 1. People would not want to read a book about radical acceptance, Elizabeth said; they would rather not imagine themselves in situations that require the practice of radical acceptance.

So, dear readers: if a mother using the word "died" or "death" offends your sensibilities (a journalist from China featured my word choice in a profile of me, which led to disapproval among Chinese readers); if you believe that "love" is a magic word that will make everything all right (as did one of my readers, who confronted me on a book tour, asking me how I could have attempted suicide if I had ever loved my children); if you think I've erred by not putting my life in the loving hands of thy god (as an ex-friend of mine believes, telling me after Vincent's death that he was sent by God and taken away by God so there was no reason for me to feel too sad); if you think suicide is too depressing a subject; if the fact that all things insoluble in life remain insoluble is too bleak for you; and if you prefer that radical acceptance remain a foreign concept to you, this is a good time for you to stop reading.

This book is about life's extremities, about facts and logic, written from a particularly abysmal place where no parent would want to be. This book will neither ask the questions you may want me to ask nor provide the closure you may expect the book to offer.

I've always refused to use the word "grieving" and I've rarely used the word "mourning"—for reasons I shall explain later. This is not a book about grieving or mourning.

This book will not provide a neat narrative arc, which some readers may hanker for: from hardship to triumph, from incomprehension to newly gained perception and wisdom, from suffering to transcendence. This book will not provide the easy satisfaction of fulfillment, inspiration, and transformation.

I've in the past quoted Montaigne: "To philosophize is to learn to die." And I now know there are other variations:

To philosophize is to learn to live with deaths.

To philosophize is to learn to live with those deaths until one dies.

To philosophize is what one can do while living in an abyss—not lost, but found.

IV

"Men Die; and They Are Not Happy."

A few months before James's death, he told me that he had been rereading *Caligula*, a play by Camus, "a bit obsessively." He had watched on the internet several productions of the play, including two in English, one in Japanese, and one in Spanish.

I had not read the play. I asked him if I should read it, knowing already that I would. He said yes. The next time I saw him—he was in college then, and would sometimes visit on Saturdays for his favorite meal, my husband's steak dinner—I told him that I was affected by a line in the play: Men die; and they are not happy.

James, in his usual understated manner, nodded with a

gentle smile. That smile, along with his quiet demeanor, were what his friends, classmates, and professors would remember in their letters to us and would mention to the reporters of the students' newspapers who would put together a stunningly beautiful tribute for him (which would put some professional journalists in two countries to shame—more on this later). I wrote to one of the student reporters after and expressed my gratitude as a mother and my admiration as a writer. The young man, a freshman at the university, replied that some of the credit should go to his two editors.

"How does one ever recover from that line?" I asked James, about the line in Camus's play. "I haven't stopped thinking about it for days."

"It's quite compelling," he said.

Men die; and they are not happy. Half of the line is a fact; the other half, a conjecture. There is no cause and effect emphasized: do men die because they are not happy, or are they not happy because they have to die someday? The two statements, existing together, are like two hands kept close, either barely touching or with their fingers intertwined.

One could envision some variations of this line:

Men die; and they are happy.

Gods don't die; and they are not happy.

Gods don't die; and they are happy.

All four scenarios offer possibilities for stories. Much of literature—one could even argue much of life, too—falls into one of the categories. There is Hamlet (men die; and they are not happy). There is Don Quixote (men die; and they are happy). And then there are those gods who dole out eternal punishments to Sisyphus, Prometheus, Narcissus, et al.: those gods, though imaginative and immortal, surely cannot be called happy.

And of course, there are plenty of mortals who take on the roles of unhappy gods. When I was very young—three or four years old—my mother invented a game in which an identical twin of mine lived in the house. That girl looked just like me but she was obedient and sweet-tempered, and she was neither selfish nor lazy. Selfishness and laziness, along with ingratitude, willfulness, and a big appetite, were my original sins. Throughout my Chinese life I was constantly reminded by my mother of these sins. In one sense and one sense only my mother was fair, as she did not attribute those flaws to my sister, who had her separate set of original sins.

Sometimes my mother recruited my sister into the game, saying that there was no point in loving me anymore because that perfect twin was in the next room. And then they would go away together, my mother laughing and talking vividly about the other girl. To this day I remember my dumbfounded panic. I was left standing next to a closet door, the top of my head not reaching the doorknob, and I was ordered not to move a step away while my mother and my sister spent time with my twin.

Once—only once—I couldn't stand the anguish, so I left the spot by the closet to look for them. That act of disobedience enraged my mother so much that years later, when I told my father about the incident, he looked agonized. He had not known what had happened, he said, but he remembered that day. He remembered listening to my crying and thinking to himself that it was not normal for a three-year-old to cry like that. Perhaps my father thought that there was something wrong with me—from an early age, my mother told family and neighbors that I was a problematic child because I was, in the Chinese phrase, "prone to feelings." Perhaps my father thought that if my mother did not direct her rage at him, it was safer to stay away from the drama. I didn't ask my father which of these hypotheses was true—but late in his life he expressed regret about not being able to protect us from our mother.

The fact that my mother, like an inventive Greek god, played that trick on me, instead of on my sister, is explained by her love for me. I'm her favored daughter: this she has made clear not only to my sister and me but to people outside the family. The last time I talked to her, in her usual tirade about my ingratitude, she said, "I've given all my love to you and for your sake, I even offended your sister. What have you given me in return?"

Perhaps gods are generally irascible, revengeful, and unpredictable. This makes the last category—*gods don't die; and they are happy*—questionable. But let us suppose there is literature to be written out of this last scenario: not only is there no death but there is the unwavering promise of everlasting happiness. Perhaps people who need euphemisms for death also need such literature, a beauteous veil to be gently draped over anything harsh or inconvenient.

I wonder what James would have said about these variations on Camus's sentence. Most possibly he would have replied with that single word, "oh," meaning, you're overthinking, or, you're going down the wrong path, or, let us each read and philosophize on our own, or, simply, please leave me alone.

After James's death, I found a picture I had taken when he was in kindergarten. When I went to pick him up, he was wearing a sign that he had written out in large print, no doubt exasperated by grown-ups asking him why he wasn't talking or telling him that he must talk:

IM NOt TaLKING Becuase I DON't WaNT TO!

My husband, referring to the picture recently, made a comment that as a family, what the four of us shared was our belief in, and our respect for, free will.

I thought for a moment and replied that despite our not knowing enough of James's thinking, what we could be certain of was this: he knew that we would respect his decision to take his own life, and he trusted that we would endure his death, as we had done it once before.

"Believe me when I say that I shall be all right. In the same strictly truthful sense that it's true that the two angles at the base of an isosceles triangle are equal. No fancy, no frill. Not symbolically, not mystically. Just all right." Richard Quin, from Rebecca West's trilogy, says this to his family before going to France during the Great War, to be instantly killed, still a teenager.

"Just all right"—these words have been on my mind in the past few months. Richard Quin shall be all right because he is crossing the English Channel to meet death, which requires nothing more of him than simply his being—being gone from this physical world, being remembered, being all right.

And yet for those who go on living, few can afford simply to be, and very few can be *all right*. The border between *all right* and *all wrong*, like the border between life and death, is not solid. For the past few months, I have replied to friends' queries with this line: "Our life is never going to be all right again, but we are doing all right."

Perhaps I should revise that statement about our belief in and our respect for free will. In the realm of being, yes, we had little regret in respecting our children's free will. But raising children is more than offering them the space to be; the world seems to care more about children's *doings* than about their *beings*. When Vincent was five, I thought of signing him up for a soccer club, and he informed me, with utter seriousness, that I would be doing that not for his happiness, but because I wanted him to be just like the other children. I instantly gave up the idea. And yet how many parents can say with confidence, when it comes to their children's upbringing, that they have achieved a real understanding between being and doing?

There was a moment that we used to talk about with laughter. In seventh grade, Vincent decided one morning that he would go to school in my dress, and went to our bedroom to look for the perfect outfit. (I do not use the word "perfect" lightly: perfectionism was part of Vincent's essence.)

My husband, with a worried look, kept offering him the dark-colored dresses: This blue one? How about this black dress? This green one would look good on you.

Vincent, in his usual flamboyant manner, picked up a pink dress. "What's the point of going to school in a dress if not a pink one?" he asked.

I explained to him that it was natural that we should worry that a pink dress might lead to bullying by his schoolmates. Vincent laughed off my concern, and said if there were idiots who dared tease him, there was all the more point in wearing pink. "Just so I can be in their face," he said.

I was full of admiration for Vincent. I felt unease, too. We parents could only do so much for our children, to raise them to be bold and free, but the world outside this bubble we called our family was often not a kind place.

Around the same time, Vincent also decided to walk home after school. It was a two-mile walk from his middle school to our house up on the hill. Half of it was along a woodsy road just off the highway, with no sidewalks or houses on either side, and it was not the safest part of Oakland. I expressed my reservations, but Vincent was a stubborn child. He promised that he would stay alert; he would run fast, he said, if needed.

Vincent was proud of his androgynous look, his long, shining black hair and his slender, crane-like physique. For two years I lived in dread of that woodsy road, where cars drove past without observing the speed limit. But a greater fear, which I never voiced to him, was that he might be abducted along that road: he might be mistaken for a pretty young girl, or there might be no mistake at all: he was a beautiful young boy.

Every semester, then and later, I would teach Grace Paley's story "Friends," and every time I would point out a passage to my students, though I doubt many of them truly understood its weight. An older woman, reminiscing about her daughter's death, says to her friends: "You know the night Abby died, when the police called me and told me? That was my first night's sleep in two years. I *knew* where she was."

For two years Vincent walked with a tube of pepper spray clasped in his hand, which once led to James's report that his classmate, having been told about Vincent's pepper spray, thought it was a condiment. That pepper spray is among the objects that have outlived Vincent. Sometimes I go into his room and take a look at it.

What can parents do but give their children the space to be, and allow them to do what they need so they can become more of themselves?

And yet, despite the parents' efforts, and despite all the beings and doings that occur as the children grow, some among them die before their time.

Children die, and they are not happy.

And their parents can never know if those children died because they were not happy, or they were not happy because they sensed, too early, that they must face their own deaths.

V

Intuitions Are Narratives

For six years before Vincent's death, I had lived with a dread that one day he might choose not to live. There were days of concern and nights of anxiety, and there were occasions for despair, but these feelings, I believed, were better kept under a calm surface. The prospect of a fire does not mean one has to carry an extinguisher on one's back around the clock.

A few times, though, I did slip into Vincent's bedroom in the middle of the night, checking that he was still there. Seeing is believing, though only to a limited extent. For six years I believed and disbelieved what I could not see at the time—but surely I was not alone in that? The ability to believe and disbelieve simultaneously seems a prerequisite for any parent. Is that rash a minor skin irritation or the first symptom of a deadly illness? Is a child's preference for playing alone a developmental stage or a sign of more serious trouble? There are many ways for things to go wrong, and yet one's hope, always, is that somehow they will turn out all right in the end. *Just all right*, we say to ourselves, out of blind courage, out of wishful thinking, both indispensable for a parent.

Should a mother rely on her intuition? And yet what's the use of intuition, in matters of life and death? A mother cannot sit in front of her child's bedroom all night long, a mother cannot follow a child's every step of life, just so that she can make sure he remains alive. A mind too reliant on intuition might easily leave reality behind. What would happen then? A mother injected a lethal drug into her own child's veins to protect him from life's threats. Another mother, plagued by postpartum depression, leaped out of the building with her newborn child. These stories in the news tend to be called tragedies, or senseless tragedies, but only a careless writer, possibly a careless writer who has never been a parent, would use those words so unthinkingly. Senseless? There is always some sense in a parent's intuitions. The real tragedy is not death itself, but a mother's difficulty in knowing when to trust her intuitions and when to let them go.

Some parents, those with no intuition and those who do not trust or understand their intuition, place their faith only in what is visible and explicable. And these self-blinded parents, by strengthening the only reality they're willing to accept, a reality without depth, ambiguity, and uncertainty, cast their children away with a centrifugal force. Think of those parents who refuse to understand their children's sexual orientation, their existential questions, or simply, their feelings. Where do those children go? To the abyss, to unreality, or, if they're lucky, to their independence.

My most humiliating writing experience took place in fourth grade. For a school writing contest, instead of turning in a patriotic essay praising the glory and beauty of our mother China, I wrote a piece decrying the hypocrisy of such contests, and then elaborating on the ugliness of life a child experienced while being forced to lie about it—"ugliness" was the word I used, more than once in that essay.

The acts of writing the essay and entering it in the contest were not done out of courage—I wasn't brave; rather, I was ten, and I was feeling suicidal despair.

It's been my experience, both as a child and as a parent, that adults—at least those specializing in arrogance and ignorance, and those who easily forget or else write off their own childhood memories—are extremely good at underestimating children. A ten-year-old already has the capacity to understand life's bleakness. Only, most ten-year-olds have not found the language to articulate their feelings, and very few of them have the ability to find a way out of that all-encompassing bleakness unaided.

Sometimes, however, a ten-year-old finds the right words. I recognized Vincent's despair when he was around the age I was when I turned in that essay; so did his fourth-grade teacher, who wrote me about the poems he had turned in for schoolwork, which were astonishingly painful and yet beautiful contemplations of life and death.

My entry in the writing contest caused a scandal among the schoolteachers. I was called to a conference room to be greeted by six or seven teachers jeering and laughing at me. An older woman, a friend of my mother's (who was also a teacher at the school), walked over and twisted my cheeks, first one and then the other, as an adult might do to an infant. She said, "You're a good student. You're not too ugly. You look like a child with some potential, but who would've thought that you could be so stupid as to write such nonsense?"

The only good thing that came out of this episode: I learned not to take reviews and criticism of my future work to heart. And I should add: my mother was in the conference room that day and laughed and jeered along with her colleagues. But when I got home from school that evening, her wrath was a story that I prefer not to remember.

When Vincent was around the same age, he asked, pointedly: "You understand suffering, and you write about suffering so well; why did you give birth to us?" A question for which I never had a good answer.

All those books teaching parents how to take care of their children—the first year, the first eighteen months, the first five or ten years—none of them addresses this difficulty: for parents and for children, the border between reality and unreality is not always clearly marked. And the most difficult fact, in my own experience as a mother and as a writer, is this: reality and unreality remain permeable.

What can a mother do, facing reality, facing unreality, but rely on her intuition while at the same time keeping her intuition at bay?

Intuitions are narratives. I have an intrinsic distrust of narratives, which are among the most misleading things in life. I have seen lives saved by narratives and lives derailed by narratives. That I've chosen to write narratives is an incongruity one has to acknowledge.

But intuitions are a tricky subset of narratives: incomplete, un-completable. I avoid putting my intuitions into words, which would be pinning a butterfly on a specimen board so as to claim the certainty of possession.

However, I did voice an intuition once. After Vincent died, Brigid reminded me that in a phone call, a few years earlier, I confessed to her that I would regard it as a triumph if I could see Vincent graduate high school. In the immediate days after his death, I had forgotten that conversation. When Brigid told me, I remembered that afternoon, making the call in my bedroom, hiding from the children because I was weeping.

Vincent had seen me cry no more than two or three times in his life; James, precisely once, a few months after Vincent died. These are facts.

Vincent did not live long enough to graduate high school. James did. These, too, are facts.

But intuitions are not facts. Intuitions, with shape-shifting qualities akin to those of paranoias or fantasies, are not always defensible, rarely unassailable.

Three days after James's birth, when we waited for the elevator on the way out of the hospital, my husband placed the carrier on the floor and knelt down beside it, listening hard to detect the newborn's breathing. Two older women walked past and admired the sight. "Now that's a first-time dad," said one to the other. We were not first-time parents. Only, like many young parents, we were beset by fears. Babies breathe on their own, but sometimes they stop breathing on their own, too.

After Vincent's death, all those questions of hows and whys and wherefores and what-ifs, which I went through in my therapist's office and in my own head, often returned me to that phone call, which Brigid reminded me of. "You knew it back then," she said.

And I was not the only one to have known it. My husband must have, too. And Vincent's therapist in California, who explained that Vincent was not a child who would take a few pills and call all his friends to announce that he was planning to kill himself. "You must be prepared," the therapist said on the phone. "If Vincent decided to do it, it would be so sudden that no one would expect it and no one could stop it."

I was not surprised when the therapist said that, just as I was not surprised when Vincent's fourth-grade teacher wrote to me about his poems. Vincent was my child; I knew—no, I felt—his despair and agitation.

I had parked the car by the roadside to pick up the therapist's call—he was returning a message I had left on his voicemail, not an emergency, not because of a crisis, but to talk about an ongoing dread. After the call, I went to pick James up from school, and later Vincent from track-and-field practice. Knowing something that may or may not happen in the future does not exempt one from the tasks of living.

Intuitions are narratives about potentials, possibilities, and alternatives. In that sense, intuitions are fiction, until, once confirmed by life, they become facts.

VI

A Framework for Living

Those moments, when intuitions remain unspoken and unspeakable, are only part of life. There are other parts of life to be lived. A mother's job is to provide a framework for living: things to do, places to go, days that never fail to break, and nights that always fall.

Once every few months we would drive to a Berkeley music shop to choose a new batch of reeds for Vincent's oboe. The shop's name is Forrests, and the first time James heard that we were going to Forrests, his five-year-old face looked anxious. What if we got lost in the forests? he asked, and it took Vincent and me a few seconds to understand James's fear. Then we all laughed because life was good at that moment, and we were not going to be lost in the forests. (And yet who among us is ever safe? "Midway upon the journey of our life / I found myself within a forest dark, / For the straightforward pathway had been lost"— even Dante did not pay attention to children's despair.)

I once found a series of numbers typed in the notes app on my phone and remembered that Vincent had been deep in a knitting project and kept calling out numbers for me to write down. What are these numbers, and in what format do I record them, I asked him, and he told me simply to write them down, as he would need me to read them back to him later. To this day I do not know what they were for, but the numbers seem reasonable, saved to perpetuity on my phone.

For some years there were three different meals to be cooked for every dinner, one for Vincent, one for James, and one for my husband and me. A mother of a classmate of James's told me that I must be crazy to go to those lengths, but I was not crazy: I simply understood the necessity of this task.

There were apples to be cored and then cut into geometrically and aesthetically pleasing slices. At a memorial service held by Vincent's old schoolmates in California, his friends brought slices of apples to share and reminisced about the apples in his lunch box, cut with absolute symmetry. That fact, in the days after Vincent's death, seemed to have vanished from my memory, and I was glad it was saved from oblivion by his friends.

The apples must be sliced perfectly, an aesthetic need of Vincent's that I grasped and agreed with, just as when I made homemade pancakes for James, I would be sure to make every piece different, and each was formed like a letter not found in the English alphabet. One must strive to live beyond the letter Z, and one must strive to go beyond one language. James would teach himself several languages: Welsh, German, Romanian, and Russian, on top of Spanish, Italian, and Japanese, the languages he took at school. His phone, I once found out by accident, was set in Lithuanian.

It seemed to me that to honor the sensitivity and peculiarity of my children—so that each could have as much space as possible to grow into his individual self—was the best I could do as a mother. Yes, I loved them, and I still love them, but more important than loving is understanding and respecting my children, which includes, more than anything else, understanding and respecting their choices to end their lives.

(Love does not guarantee understanding or respect. I cannot challenge my mother's claim that she's loved me more than she's loved anyone—more than she's loved my sister and my father, but perhaps not more than she's loved herself. "You love your children more than you love me" was a complaint she made when my children were young. Two years after Vincent died, she informed me that there was some karma in my losing a child: I had failed to return her love for me.)

Things to do, places to go, a framework for living is a framework for memory.

James was given his first Gmail account at three. After a quarrel with Vincent, he asked for my help in creating an email account for himself. "Dear Vincent: You are a mini," James wrote, mistyping "meanie" as "mini," though observing the etiquette of proper correspondence. In those days, whenever I was out of town, I would write a stack of cards ahead of time so my husband could include a card for each day of my absence in James's lunch box. All those cards were signed "Love, Mommy." Moments after Vincent received the email, they reconciled, as Vincent was amused that James's "hate email" ended with "Love, James."

In the Reina Sofía Museum in Madrid, James, at three, fell asleep in my arms. I sent my husband to see artwork while I taught Vincent people watching, my favorite hobby. We sat on a bench in the long corridor, trying to find something special in each person walking past us. After a while, Vincent pointed out this baffling fact: groups of three tended to be composed of two old women with one old man—or two young men with one young woman. "You see, it's never two old men with one old woman or two young women with one young man," Vincent said. "Why is that?"

Why had I never noticed?

Vincent, at five, read a biography of Vincent van Gogh for children. He said to James: "Vincent van Gogh's little brother Theo supported him as an artist. James, when we grow up, will you support me as an artist?" James, not yet three, nodded fullheartedly. A few years later, I overheard Vincent talking to his best friend. "When I grow up, I need to find a good job because I need to support James." I told Vincent that we wanted him to live his own life, as James would be not his responsibility, but ours. He tolerated me for a moment and then pointed out, very reasonably, that it was not as though we parents would live forever. "After you and Daddy die, I will have to support James," he said.

Two years after Vincent died, I went to the Van Gogh Museum in Amsterdam and was surprised to learn that Theo had lived for only six more months after Vincent's death. That fact revisited me after James's death.

My friend Edmund read me a poem he'd recently written, about three moments of happiness in his life. He said that somewhere he'd read that each person had only three real happy memories. Could that be true? Afterward, I started to record in my notebooks the moments I'd been happy with Vincent and James, and I quickly got past three.

If I focus my mind on the happy moments, the framework for living seems sturdy enough. And yet it is not an indestructible shelter from catastrophes. A mother dedicating herself to the framework for living is like a shipbuilder building a vessel, not asking if the voyage is to be through calm seas or tempests, not questioning if there will be a tomorrow or not.

Seeing is believing, but a mother must restrain herself from *foreseeing*. To foresee is to give too much weight to intuition; foreseeing might be waving a white flag prematurely.

VII

So Much for a Mother's Intuitions

Vincent's death did not come as a complete surprise, but it was a never-healing wound. It was not, however, a wound inflicted by him or his decision. Once, at an event for a mental health institute in Los Angeles, a psychiatrist interviewing me pressed me and asked if I felt any anger toward Vincent. He said he could detect no anger in the book I had written for Vincent. He told me that earlier in his career, he'd lost a teenage patient to suicide, and he could still feel the lingering anger years later.

He is not the only person who has asked me about anger: the question must be relevant and legitimate, but anger is not a major or even a minor emotion in my life. I explained this to the doctor in Los Angeles, and he said I was "very fortunate." I believed him—I have known some angry people, I have encountered many people's anger, but I have rarely found angry people illuminating or inspiring. Too often their anger—a feeling, a reaction, an interpretation—is presented as fact, or, worse, truth.

I did not feel any anger when Vincent died—not at him, not at life, either. But I did feel baffled and wounded by life. That a mother could do all things humanly possible and sensible for a child but still could not keep him alive—this was the fact that I would have to live with, I thought, every single day, for the rest of my life. It was Vincent's death that made me begin to use that phrase, "every single day, for the rest of my life."

After Vincent's death, there were excruciating days, days of numbness, days of contentment, and days of melancholy, days of reading and writing and days of not being able to read or write, days of holding on upside down (like the bat in Marianne Moore's poem) and days of holding on with the right side up. But in all those days, where one is obliged to live ("where can we live but days?" in Philip Larkin's words), there remained that thought: every single day, for the rest of my life, I will be thinking of Vincent.

I had not lived with the same dread for James when he was alive. My parental anxiety about him was largely about his future. Then one day, he walked out of the world in the same way as Vincent did.

"There is no good way to say this. We're very sorry for your loss." The police came and then left swiftly, as though they were actors coming onto stage to deliver their lines and, having done so, exiting the stage right away.

I texted Brigid and then texted my therapist, telling them that James had died from suicide. Later, they both told me their initial reactions, which were similar.

"I knew every one of those words in the message but I didn't understand what those words meant, put together," Brigid said. Half an hour before I sent that text to her, I had been on the phone with her, and James had been in our lighthearted conversation.

My therapist said that when he read the message, his initial thought was that "it made no sense, it made no sense at all."

James died on Friday, and the Saturday before that was the last time Brigid had seen him (the last time for us, too). He was home from college for a meal on New Year's Day of the lunar calendar, and Brigid noticed his good spirits and his composure. A week or two before his death, my therapist had asked me (not for the first time) if I worried about James feeling suicidal, and I had enough confidence to say that, even though one could never say no to that possibility with certainty, I didn't really think he was suicidal.

So much for a mother's intuitions.

And yet one wonders, in retrospect, what prompted the conversation about the probability or improbability of James feeling suicidal, which had been a reoccurring topic in the therapist's office. Was it intuition or paranoia that led to the discussion shortly before James died—a premonition I couldn't explain? It doesn't matter, as the facts remain irrefutable: I did not anticipate that James would choose suicide; I did not detect any sign.

For six years before Vincent's death, I lived in dread of that possibility. For six years between the two boys' deaths, James, too, was pondering suicide, Vincent's, and then, at some point, his own. I did not know when that shift happened; I did not even think that shift would happen, as I worried only about James's life, not about his death.

Two months after Vincent died, James asked for my copy of *Anna Karenina*. I hesitated although I had never worried about what my children were reading. They were both precocious readers and I let them explore all the literature available to them. I asked James, who was then in seventh grade, if he knew that by the end of *Anna Karenina*, Anna committed suicide. He said yes. I then asked him if he wanted to read the novel because of that, and he only smiled his gentle smile.

I gave the book to him, and it had become one of the books we talked about on and off for the next few years.

Tolstoy's characters are easily vexed, or maybe the Russians are easily vexed—he told me a few days into his reading. That the words "vex" and "vexation" appear often in the text is an observation I will always remember and treasure. James saw himself in Levin, as I had expected, though I did point out that Levin was often vexed while he—James—was rarely vexed. He adored Kitty; he was fond of Anna's brother, Stiva (because he was immoral *and* genuine); and he found Vronsky the most complex character in the novel. What about Anna, I said, and James thought for a while, then said that Anna brought tragedies onto herself *and then* complained about them. I now wish I had asked him which of those two he had found more troubling: that she brought tragedies onto herself, or that she complained. We did not discuss her suicide.

I reread *Anna Karenina* while writing this book. I had forgotten that before Anna's suicide, there was Vronsky's attempt. He shoots himself, impulsively and perhaps not entirely fullheartedly, out of desperate love for Anna. Overshadowed by Anna's death, this episode had been blocked out in my memory. I wish I had discussed this with James.

A few weeks before his death, James told me that he was reading *The Myth of Sisyphus* by Camus, and I said that I'd read the book too when I was in college. After that conversation, I reread the opening pages of the book:

"There is but one truly serious philosophical problem, and that is suicide. Judging whether life is or is not worth living amounts to answering the fundamental question of philosophy."

Did I have a fleeting thought that I should have checked in with James to see if he felt suicidal? I can't answer that question now, because on this side of death no answer can be trusted.

When we dropped James off at his dorm after that last dinner with us, I asked him what he was reading, and he replied that he was rereading *The Myth of Sisyphus*. Then he stepped out of the car and raised a hand. James was a person of few words and even fewer gestures. That raised hand, like that versatile single word "oh" in his conversation, could mean many things: Hello, or goodbye, or leave me alone, or thank you, or, simply a reply to the words I said when he stepped out of the car, "I love you, James."

Through their entire lives, at every school drop-off, every time they were leaving for a party or a playdate, every time I was leaving for a trip, and with each exchange of text, the last thing I said to Vincent and James was inevitably "I love you."

No matter how long we get to parent our children, there are only limited numbers of "I love yous" we can say to them. That, too, is a fact.

VIII

Children Die, and Parents Go on Living

That Friday, after the police left, the phone calls came in. I've learned the necessity of changing behavior after a sudden death. I never pick up phone calls from unknown numbers, but in those next few days they were the only calls I would pick up: death would bring strangers into our world, while friends would be put on hold. All those calls from unknown numbers were priorities because they were about James—no, not about James, but about the practical matters after his death.

My husband and I were stunned, astonished, shocked, or any of the words one uses in such a situation. The truth was, we, like Brigid and my therapist (and my husband's therapist), could not immediately do anything with this fact. It was ushering in a new reality, which we could neither enter nor ignore. James, ahead of us, was already in that new reality.

I remember, after taking a phone call from the university, sitting down next to my husband, who had not moved from the end of the sofa for hours that evening, and saying in a quiet voice, heard only by myself, "Shit."

I don't swear, I don't scream out in pain, I don't smash plates or bowls, I don't bang doors or punch walls. I have always known that I can keep my body still and my mind clear, a skill that I must have mastered from being the daughter of my mother, who had done all the screaming and banging and crying and swearing when I was growing up. A few days after James died, I remembered once again my mother's wrath when she whipped my shoulders and back with a metal pencil box or a broomstick, not because I had done anything unforgivable, but because she was angry. The longer she beat me, the angrier she became, because I was neither crying nor trying to escape her beating. "I just don't believe I can't make you cry," she would swear, hitting out of a blind rage. I would sit in the chair, wooden-faced and dry-eyed, knowing that other than exhausting herself, there was nothing she could do to claim victory over me.

Life has stunned me, but I prefer not to give life the

pleasure of boasting that it has defeated me, just as I did not give my mother the satisfaction of knowing that her beating could break me and bring tears to my eyes.

So when I sat down next to my husband and said "Shit," that unfamiliar word was life at an extremity, to which I responded with my own extremity. Sometimes I wonder if that might have been the worst moment in my life, though, as Edgar said in *King Lear*, "And worse I may be yet. The worst is not / So long as we can say 'This is the worst.'"

A few years ago, a young woman spent two days with me for a profile for *The New York Times*, and for that interview (as for all the other interviews), I made it clear that I would not answer questions about my husband and James. After James's death, in a message to me, she referred to that instinct of mine to respect James's privacy and to protect him. Once again, the thought occurred to me that a mother can do all things humanly possible for a child and cannot keep him alive.

Parents die, and children go on living. It is statistically sound to say that this is the case for the majority of the population.

But sometimes children die before their parents.

Children die, and parents go on living. Those parents go on living because they do not have many options: they either live or follow their children down to Hades.

Children die, and parents go on living. Those parents go on living because death, though a hard, hard thing, is not always the hardest thing. Both my children chose a hard thing. We are left with the hardest: to live after their deaths.

Sometimes a young writer or a writing student tells me how hard they find writing is. Writing is so hard, they say, with a whine or else self-glorification in their voice. That always puts me in a suspicious mood. If you complain about writing being hard—I sometimes want to say to them—then you must have understood very little about life.

Writing is hard, but living is harder. Writing is optional. Living, too, is optional, though its demands make writing seem idyllic.

A few weeks after James died, I was home alone and heard a vehicle pull into the driveway. Then I heard a car door open and close, then men talking. My thought at that instant was that the police were here again, this time telling me that my husband had died.

It was a deliveryman who was loudly chatting with another man on speakerphone.

When Vincent and James were in elementary school, the mother of three of their school friends died from suicide. The three boys were eight, six, and four years old. A few days after, they were at their grandmother's when she picked up a phone call. "Oh no," she exclaimed when the person on the other end said something.

All three boys perked up and asked in unison, "Is Daddy dead?"

Dying is hard. Living is harder. Even harder is living on when life is fractured by timeless deaths. It takes an instant for death to become a fact, a single point in a time line, which eclipses all things in the past and eliminates any possibility for the future. Death is like Euclid's definition of the point in geometry: "A point is that which has no part."

Living, on the other hand, is not about a single point. There is not a single point in time or space that can become life itself.

Children die, and parents go on living. Those parents go on living because that's the only way for them to go on loving their children, whose deaths easily turn them into a news story one day and gossip the next day, and then, eventually, statistics.

Children die, and parents go on living, except they go on living in a different way than they did before. It's like living with "a new knowledge of reality," I wrote to my friend Deborah a couple of weeks after James's death, quoting the last line of the last poem of the collected poems of Wallace Stevens, titled "Not Ideas About the Thing but the Thing Itself."

IX

A New Knowledge of Reality

And yet this new knowledge of reality is not entirely new, this reality is not unknown to us.

That Friday, after the police left, there was the déjà vu that kept me immobile, but for no more than a minute. We'd done it once, and we would have to do it all over again, without any corners to cut, and yet with a few things remembered and a few skills mastered.

Vincent died on a Thursday, when I was out of town. Not knowing he had died, but suspecting that he had, I left Amherst, Massachusetts, half an hour after arriving there, but traffic from Massachusetts to New Jersey on that day was endlessly congested. The two detectives from

Princeton, who had been waiting for me since half past four with my husband and James, discussed, at some point, the possibility of having highway patrol intercept me on the border of Connecticut and New York in order to escort me back in a police vehicle. They decided against it, my husband told me, because they worried that I might have a breakdown. In that case, the police would have no option but to send me to a hospital to be sedated.

I arrived in Princeton at half past nine, talked to the detectives, talked to my husband, and then went upstairs to see James. He must have sensed it, my husband told me, but he had been waiting for my return to tell James. "You may have guessed this," I said to him when he allowed me to sit on his bed and hold his hands. "I'm so sorry, James, but Vincent died this afternoon from suicide."

Neither of us cried, but I remember thinking James was wilting, and I was wilting too. We might have sat together for ten or twenty minutes, or an hour. At some point, I let in our dog so James could cuddle with him.

For a few weeks after Vincent's death, James, though a quiet child, was chatty with Quintus. "I huggie thee, Quintus," he would say to the dog every time he came into the house, and the combination of the babyish language with the archaic English was a sign, I knew, of James's anguish. From an early age, he talked in an extremely articulate manner with sophisticated vocabulary; "professorial," a doctor observed in her assessment of him. For James, child-ish phrases or words, like that single swear word for me, were reactions to life's extremity. The only time he saw me cry, after Vincent's death, he looked pained. "Why cry you?" he asked ungrammatically. I said I was crying because I felt sad. "Why you sad?" he asked, and I replied that I was sad for him and for Quintus and for us and I was particu-larly sad for Vincent.

Quintus was named by Vincent, "the fifth" in Latin, because when he arrived we had four members in the family. After Vincent died, James's Californian therapist, who Skyped that fall and winter once a week to support James (and us), told me that one day James had explained to him matter-of-factly that Quintus was thus named be-cause there had been four people in the family. He—the therapist—felt the poignancy of this moment because James did not say that one of those four people had died. He only looked his stoic self, the therapist said.

Of course, we've always been a household of four people for James. That was the condition he was born into. Death would not change that for him, just as two deaths do not change it for me: when I think of my family now, I think of us as two parents, two children, and a dog.

Quintus joined the family at eight weeks old when Vincent was ten and James seven. Now an old dog, Quin-tus moves gingerly on the stairs. Sometimes he bumps into the furniture and looks sheepishly embarrassed. His joints are stiff and his eyes are nearly entirely clouded by cataracts.

Two months after Vincent's death, I packed up his clothes for the move to the house he would not live in. Quintus lingered around the whole time, sniffing the suitcases. "Do you want a brother, Quintus?" I once heard James ask. They were both lying down on the carpeted landing. We had just moved into the house.

After James moved into the college dorm, any small noise upstairs would make Quintus, who is not keen to climb stairs, rush up to check James's bedroom or his playroom. But in the past few weeks, Quintus seems to have gotten used to this new reality. He only goes to James's rooms when I go there. Oblivion is a kind of blessing, too, though one I would prefer not to have to experience.

For weeks I have been trying to remember where Quintus was when the police came to tell us about James. I could place everyone in that scene, but Quintus was not around. He must have gone back to his bed.

Children die, and their dog goes on living.

The night after Vincent died, I sat up all night, not daring to lie down. I dreaded sleep, for fear that when the morning arrived, there would be a brief moment—no more than ten seconds—when what had happened and what had not happened seemed interchangeable. I dreaded that plummeting from not remembering to remembering. I would rather stay awake all night so there was no mistake, no illusion, only the abyss from where I could not fall further.

Death is one reality, life is another. The two realities are rarely compatible. Sometimes one reality obliterates the other, or, worse, banishes the other into the realm of unreality. I remembered texting Brigid that night, asking her to always remind me of this cold, cold fact—that Vincent died—if ever I were not to believe it.

The saddest and yet the most irrefutable truth: when you lose a second child, you have already learned a few things about losing a child from your previous experience.

The second time around I knew neither to battle life nor to battle death: in both endeavors, there would be unlimited exhaustion and very little to gain. If death is one reality and life is another, I would rather they were like two hands placed next to each other—barely touching or with fingers intertwined. The two hands are not arm wrestling; they cannot beat or dominate each other.

I called Brigid and asked if she could come to Princeton right away. "We need someone other than the two of us in the house," I said to her, "so we don't slip into unreality." Shortly after she arrived, I went to bed. I did not dread sleep. In fact, I knew I needed all the sleep I could get so as to face the rest of my life.

Between the phone call to Brigid and her arrival, I saw that the university had sent the news out by email to the community. I wrote immediately to my friend Christiane, who taught James in her linguistics class the previous semester, and who was among a handful of adults in James's life, other than his parents, who had some sense of James's essence.

Christiane wrote back right away: " I saw the news and have been agonizing over what to say to you. If there is anything I can do to ease your pain, let me know. You did everything you could to help James find his place in life, but he wanted to leave and one must let go. I, too, was unable to reach him in my very limited way, and I am devastated."

You did everything you could to help James find his place in life, but he wanted to leave and one must let go—for weeks and months after, I've often returned to Christiane's words, and to her extraordinary instinct to write in this way at that most difficult moment, from a deep and austere understanding of James, of his parents, and of life itself. Very few people, in my experience, have the moral courage to say what Christiane said to me on that day, precisely an hour and a half after a child's death.

X

Another Kind of Newborn

The morning after James's death, I wrote to my agent Sarah—"I feel deeply stunned and wounded by life"—then reread it and deleted the adverb "deeply," which was an extraneous word. It seemed as though it was only days earlier that I had written to Sarah about Vincent, the morning after his death. Brigid, who was sitting next to me and drafting an email to a list of friends that I asked her to write on our behalf, later reported my friend Maile replying that, for a moment, she thought Brigid had accidentally sent an email from an old draft, and the news was about Vincent, not James.

It was five o'clock when Brigid and I sat in the kitchen,

writing the emails. After what felt like a long time, I looked at the clock. It was still not yet six o'clock. There were people to call, and arrangements to make, but the day was slow to break. I remembered the other time, sitting at the kitchen counter myself, on the morning after Vincent died: then, too, it seemed that the clock had stopped at five o'clock.

When life is full of tasks, obligations, and events, time carries us, too swiftly it seems, for is it not our perpetual protest about life that there is not enough time for this or that? But those who complain about that—myself at different phases of my life, too—forget how fortunate they are: Life does not guarantee that time has the capacity to carry us. Time flies, time is fleeting, but then there comes a moment when time, no longer nimble-footed, no longer winged, is for us to carry.

Death, a major disruptor of life, can feel like a black hole, depleting all one's energy, but death fails to be a black hole in one particular sense: it does not absorb all the time. Those who have to live through the days after a beloved's death and those who are beset by debilitating depression will know this: time stands still, time feels monotonous, and then time becomes Sisyphus's boulder. One carries it from morning to night, and if sleep comes, it's but meager comfort with little relief. Then, one starts all over again the next day. The exhaustion one feels while mourning or battling depression is from that never-ending effort to carry time, an exhaustion similar to that of carrying an infant that refuses to nurse, refuses to fall asleep, and cries all day long. One cannot drop time as one cannot drop a baby; one simply has to *carry* on.

The immediate days after a child's death (or the death of any loved one, I think) share something with the immediate days after a child's birth. Very rarely in life do we count the days as loyally as we count a newborn's beginnings: a day old, three days old, seven days old, two weeks old, three weeks old—in fact, the only other time the days are counted in such a consistent and mindful manner, in my experience, is after the death of a child: one day gone, three days gone, a week gone, three months gone.

And the days, counted so closely, with all those hours and minutes for one to carry, feel simultaneously long and fleeting. One nurses a baby, changes his diaper, holds him until he falls asleep, puts him down in a bassinet or a crib, and picks him up again because a baby is good at startling himself. If one is lucky, one has the time to nap a little before the baby needs a diaper change and the next nursing. One is exhausted, from sleep deprivation, from the inexperience of taking care of a new human being, from cracked nipples and chronically injured wrists, from the wounds from the cesarean section or vaginal tearing, all slow to heal.

And still the days go so fast, and maternity leave is over in no time.

I took six weeks off after Vincent's birth. I was working in a hospital lab at the time and this was the maternity leave allowed. For the next eight months, Vincent, refusing to take pumped breast milk from a bottle, would not eat between eight a.m. and five p.m., and from five p.m. onward, when I got home, he would nurse once an hour, all night long, to stock up for the next day. Did I sleep at all during those months? Amazed and awed by Vincent's stubbornness, I lived in a dream. And Vincent thrived as an infant, and that was all that mattered to a mother.

I was in graduate school at Iowa Writers' Workshop when I gave birth to James. When he was a week old, I went back to teaching as a graduate instructor, with James in a carrier. I went back to taking Marilynne Robinson's class with James sleeping in a sling. That spring, everyone joked that James Li was the only person who dared interrupt Marilynne.

One does not master the skills of taking care of a baby by reading a manual or taking a few classes. One fumbles and blunders, never certain if one has done everything right. One weeps from exhaustion or frustration, and one worries and loses sleep over anything, small or large. There was Vincent's fever—which landed him in NICU at three days old. There was James's seizure at two years old—when an ambulance sped us through Oakland. There was Vincent's perceived speech delay when he was two and a half: not a word, not even meaningful babbling, though after I went away for a short trip, I returned to find Vincent singing ABCs, counting effortlessly, and speaking long and complete sentences. Children take their own time—how many times are new parents told this by more experienced people, and yet who among them can ever find assurance in that cliché? The parents' job is to doubt and to worry. When James was two and a half and had not yet shown any aptitude for potty training, I shared my anxiety with his two preschool teachers, and they laughed and pointed out that since James could read fluently in a diaper, they were not worried themselves. They told me that another teacher in the preschool believed that James memorized all the picture books rather than truly being able to read, so James's teachers gave him a memo from the president of the college with which the preschool was affiliated. James read the memo from beginning to end, not, perhaps, understanding much of the administrative business.

How did you learn to read? we asked James, and he said Vincent taught him—though how true that statement was was questionable. When Vincent was six, he asked James if he knew how a man and a woman made a baby. James said, rather too matter-of-factly: "A man puts his penis in a woman's vagina. Then a sperm and an egg get together. That will make a baby." Vincent, surprised, asked James how he had learned that, and James replied that it was on page 76 of the *Encyclopedia of the Human Body*.

The worries, the frustrations, the joys, the surprises—parents rarely know enough about parenting, and yet children, somehow, offer parents the assistance they need; they help themselves grow up.

The death of a child is a newborn, too. The death of a child is a newborn that does not grow or change. And those children, gone from the world, are no longer able to help their parents.

XI

Abyss as a Habitat

A mother gives birth to a firstborn, and blunders through the baby's infanthood. Then she gives birth to another baby. The second time things are somewhat familiar, less daunting, and yet just as many things can go wrong.

Losing a child for the second time, I knew some things to be important: sleep, hydration, small and frequent snacks, daily exercise. Get out of bed at the regular time and never ruminate while lying in bed. Make the effort to brew good coffee in the morning. Read—one act of Shakespeare is good enough, so is a page of Euclid's geometry, a chapter of Henry James's biography, or one poem from

Wallace Stevens's collection. Write—there is no reason to stop working and there is also no reason to strive for regular working hours. Anything that prevents agitation or rumination is good for the mind. And, most important of all, for me: radical acceptance. The death of a child realigns time and space. If an abyss is where I shall be for the rest of my life, the abyss is my habitat. One should not waste energy fighting one's habitat.

I have only this abyss, which is my life. And an inevitable part of existing in this abyss is exhaustion, which the second time I learned to accept without protest. My friend Edmund told me that after his Swiss lover died, he felt like one of those women hauling heavy laundry out of a river, all day long, never ending. It seems a beloved's death makes one a Sisyphus, too. After James died, flowers arrived in front of our door. The flowers deserved attention, but I had to turn myself inside out to find the energy needed for that attention: to cut open the packaging, to trim a bouquet of peonies, to place them in a vase. (Here's a small thing I've learned: if one is to send flowers as a gesture of condolence, better to ensure the flowers arrive already arranged in a vase.)

In that exhaustion, still there is some living to do. What was beyond my capacity I would not aspire to accomplish, so I asked my agents and Brigid to help me cancel travel and public events for the next few months. What was within my capacity I would not shy away from, as work is as essential as breathing and sleeping. I was at the beginning of a nearly yearlong process of judging a prize, and I decided to remain on the judging panel, a decision my intuition told me was the right one and one that the experience itself has confirmed: the reading has offered a structure for my days, and the monthly meetings with the other judges have taken place in a realm that is independent of my personal life.

And there was a novel-in-progress that I had been working on for several months. "On the way here I wondered if you would have to take some time off from it," Brigid said the day after James died, when I told her that I intended to keep working on the novel. "And knowing you, of course you would not."

I did not stop writing or take time off from teaching when Vincent died. Writing, teaching, gardening, grocery shopping, cooking, doing laundry—all these activities are time-bound, and they do not compete with my children, who are timeless now. There is no rush, as I will have every single day, for the rest of my life, to think about Vincent and James, outside time, outside the many activities of everyday life.

And this, among other reasons, is why I am against the word "grief," which in contemporary culture seems to indicate a process that has an end point: the sooner you get there, the sooner you prove yourself to be a good sport at living, and the less awkward people around you will feel. Sometimes people ask me where I am in the grieving process, and I wonder whether they understand anything at all about losing someone. How lonely the dead would feel, if the living were to stand up from death's shadow, clap their hands, dust their pants, and say to themselves and to the world, I am done with my grieving; from this point on it's life as usual, business as usual.

I don't want an end point to my sorrow. The death of a child is not a heat wave or a snowstorm, nor an obstacle race to rush through and win, nor an acute or chronic illness to recover from. What is grief but a word, a shortcut, a simplification of something much larger than that word?

Thinking about my children is like air, like time. Thinking about them will only end when I reach the end of my life.

The only passage in which grief appears in its truest meaning is from *King John*, when Constance speaks eloquently of a grief that is called madness by others in the play.

> Grief fills the room up of my absent child,
> Lies in his bed, walks up and down with me,
> Puts on his pretty looks, repeats his words,
> Remembers me of all his gracious parts,

Stuffs out his vacant garments with his form;
Then, have I reason to be fond of grief?
Fare you well. Had you such a loss as I,
I could give better comfort than you do.
I will not keep this form upon my head
When there is such disorder in my wit.

Have I reason to be fond of grief? Yes, as much as a
mother has reason to love her children. Alas, few people
use the word "grief" these days as compellingly as Constance. For that reason, I prefer that in the abyss that is my
habitat, grief is not given a place by design. If it decides to
grow there, it will grow like a volunteer rose campion or a
sweet violet or a columbine.

XII

Things in Nature Merely Grow

Late last year, I planted twelve hundred bulbs, an addition to the seven hundred and the five hundred from the previous two autumns. The tender green had just been popping out of the stale, winter-long snow when James died, and by late March the bulbs were blooming with abandon. Things in nature merely grow—the line has become a reoccurring thought after James's death—things in nature merely grow until it's time for them to die.

I began to garden when we moved into the house where Vincent had said he would help me improve the garden. Gardening takes time and energy, and things go wrong more often than they go right. Wild animals and pests are abundant in the New Jersey countryside: squirrels, ground-hogs, rabbits, moles, voles, Japanese beetles, and deer. The weather is not always friendly: a late spring snowstorm killed off a season of hydrangea one year, and excessive heat baked a flush of roses another year. And yet why raise a fist and protest against weather and wild creatures: they are part of nature, too, like the robins that each spring build a nest in one of the rosebushes, or the wrens making a home in the small birdhouses I hang in the garden specif-ically for them, or the hummingbirds and the swallowtails busy in the flowers, a mesmerizing, joyful sight.

Years ago, when we moved into our first house in Cal-ifornia, William Trevor wrote to encourage me to start a garden. When he and his wife, Jane, moved to the Devon countryside, he told me, there had not been a garden there, and decades later, the garden, growing too big for the aged couple, "takes up what time there is." He talked about re-ducing the size of the garden and returning part of it to the sheep.

But that house up in the Oakland hills was in the woods, so there was not enough sunlight, and my children were young then, and I didn't seem to have the time. Now that I have a garden, I've come to understand Trevor's point: gardening is good training for a novelist. One learns to be patient, one learns to make concessions, one learns to redefine one's visions and ambitions, and one learns to stop being a perfectionist. A garden is good training for life, too. Would it have changed Vincent a little, had he had the opportunity to work on the garden with me for a season, several seasons? Better stop asking these questions that tread in the realm of alternatives—whatever the answer is doesn't make a difference in this life.

And one must garden as realistically as one lives after the deaths of one's children. One must, especially, refrain from giving the flowers and plants metaphorical or symbolic meaning beyond nature's mere way of being. After James died, someone sent me a picture of spring flowers and touted "earth's regenerative power." That kind of language, like the encouragement from people who cheerfully predicted that I would soon reach "the end of the tunnel," makes me conscious of how people fall into the trap of using clichés to express care.

Clichés are not merely flabby words used to express unimaginative thoughts; rather, clichés corrode the mind. Flabby language begetting flabby thinking seems a more alarming prospect than the opposite, flabby thinking finding refuge in flabby language.

My garden is not a metaphor for hope or regeneration, the flowers are never tasked to be the heralds for brightness and optimism. Things in nature merely grow. There is no suicidal or angry rose, there is no depressed or rebellious lily. Plants have but one goal: to live. In order to live they grow when they can, and go into dormancy if needed. They live until they die—and either they die as destined by nature or are cut down by other elements in nature. A garden is a placeholder. Flowers are placeholders.

For twenty years, ever since Brigid started to read and edit my work, the word "placeholder" has become an essential concept of my philosophy. Often she underlines a passage and tells me that a sentence is a placeholder for a real sentence, or that a thought is still at a place-holding stage, waiting for a clearer thought to emerge in sharper words.

Much of what one does in life is to hold a place for something and to uphold a space for someone. Cooking—for a family of four, then for a family of three, and now for my husband and myself—is making time as concrete as possible, seven days a week. When James was in third grade, a school project required a cereal box, and his friend Jason, concerned that James had never eaten cereal in his life, told his mother that they must provide James with a cereal box so he did not fail his project. Do you want cereal for breakfast, I asked James, telling him that I didn't mean to deprive him of cereal; that, he replied, would be a sad breakfast. James so rarely used adjectives to describe feelings that I noticed that word "sad" in his reply: if I was limited as a mother, I would nonetheless make sure his breakfast would never be called sad.

Years ago, after a mental crisis, I stayed in an emergency facility in California for a weekend. At mealtimes, patients lined up to receive trays of mushy, nondescript food, and the man or the woman who handed over the tray would say, "Here, made with love, just for you." That sentence, along with the police detectives' line—there is no good way to say this—is among the saddest words ever said to me.

So all of Vincent's favorite dishes, which I stopped making after his death; all of James's favorites dishes, which I stopped making after his death; all those pancakes shaped beyond the letter Z—still one must prevail, looking for new recipes, trying different colors and textures on a plate, making every detail count in a meal as one makes every word count in writing. I would not, however, say that these meals are "made with love." "Love" is one of those words that, though meaningful to the utmost degree, is meaningless in much of its daily use. I would say these meals are "made with care."

And parenting—is that not the ultimate effort to hold a place for children, so that, to the best of one's ability, they can be given all they need to grow? And yet there is futility, too, in this effort: the children are bound to outgrow the space the parents provide; the world is just outside. A mother can cook every meal with great care, but a mother's care, like a point in geometry, is essential to the order of things, insubstantial in the scale of things.

I keep a stack of notebooks on my desk. One notebook is never enough, as different moods and different readings demand their own notebooks; the scribblings are but "words, words, words," as Hamlet says, and which I sometimes say to myself when I am in the middle of a project, questioning the point of a book. I feel comforted when Elizabeth says this happens to her, too, with every book she writes.

While working on this book—"the book for James"—I had a moment of diffidence, feeling that the complaint of "words, words, words" came to me from James. We did not hold a memorial service for James, as we had done for Vincent—it would have been the last thing James wanted, to be at the center of anything, to be remembered publicly, to be put in a position that violated his essence—James, true to Brigid's observation, is the antithesis of many things.

"A book can be more than just a gesture toward the subject of the book," Elizabeth said to me, very helpfully, when I expressed my doubt.

A book is a placeholder, no more, no less. This book for James—what does it hold? All the words that have come to me: many of them fall short; some are kept because they are needed to hold a place for James.

These days, I am conscious of the placeholders in my life, all of them reminders of what I feel—that combination of keen attention and profound indifference, that mixture of intense emotion and an equally intense apathy. Writing a sentence again and again until it feels right is a placeholder. Comparing the hues and scents of two roses on the same branch—one just open, one past its prime—is a placeholder. Spending a few extra minutes to make a vinaigrette with fresh figs and the basil I've grown is a placeholder. Reading Anne Carson's rendition of Hekabe's extremity—"What shall I cry? What howl shall I howl?"—and thinking about the shadow of those words in Lear's "Howl, howl, howl, howl!"; listening to the "Flower Duet," one of Vincent's favorites (he was the one to introduce the opera *Lakmé* to me), or listening to some Gilbert and Sullivan songs, which James's piano and singing teacher had taught him when he was in grade school, as a way to bring him out of his silence; looking at the old traveling pictures, thinking about but not touching Vincent's clothes in his closet, thinking about but not being able to unpack James's suitcase brought back from his dorm— every action is a placeholder, so is every action not taken. What I did for my children once made placeholders of their lives; what I couldn't do—keep them alive—is the most important placeholder of my life: my children, in their absence.

Vincent lived feelingly. James lived thinkingly. When Vincent died, I was able to conjure him up in a book by feeling, but I knew, right after James died, that I would not be able to do that for him. James would not like a book written from feelings.

The day after James's death, I told Brigid that to live up to his standards, I must try to live thinkingly; to live according to logic, to facts, and to live in radical acceptance. When she asked me to elaborate, I could not find the words to expand my statement. But I may have a better answer for her question now: to live only with meaningful placeholders and to acknowledge that they are nevertheless only placeholders.

Because placeholders are neither solutions nor salvations. None of them will play the magic trick of delivering me into another realm, where life regenerates itself through hope and love and wishful thinking. Neither my garden nor my writing will solve what is insoluble in my life. Though there are not that many things in my life that are worthy of that adjective, "insoluble."

The only insoluble matter, before this past February, was Vincent: he would never be back to be among us, to entertain us with his wit and fantasy, to pressure us to go further in our thinking with his endless questioning. In a piece I published in *The New Yorker*, about gardening and Vincent, there are two paragraphs that read differently today:

One early summer morning, I looked out the window and saw two deer and a rabbit in my front garden, eating up some hydrangea bushes I had planted a few weeks earlier. It occurred to me that, had I been able to go back to my childhood self and tell her that one day I would live in a place where rabbits and deer eat side by side peacefully, the child would be incredulous: certainly no real people could live in a fairy tale like that?

"I am sure that if you had been told when you were a child about all the things that you were going to have to do, you would have thought you had better die at once, you would not have believed you could ever have the strength to do them." In West's trilogy, Richard Quin says this to his mother before he leaves to be killed in France. Had I been able to go back to my childhood self and tell her that one day I would live as a mother who has lost a son, the child would be equally incredulous: surely such things happen only in fiction, to characters who are much more interesting and tragic?

James, who graduated from high school in his blue cap and gown, was still kept safe in the bubble that was called last year when the piece was published. Had I been able to go back and tell myself that in six months I would live as a mother who has lost two sons, the novelist in me and the mother in me would have been equally incredulous. That wouldn't do, in fiction or in life. I would have raised my voice and protested: that only happens in Greek tragedies.

The chorus, singing about Herakles's children, who would soon be killed by Herakles in a frenzy of madness, admonishes (in Anne Carson's translation): "Bad luck is not gone from these children, but neither is beauty."

Before we went to James's high school graduation, I asked him if he would give me permission to make a bouquet of flowers from my garden and present it to him at the ceremony. He declined, as I knew he would. At the ceremony many of his schoolmates took selfies and then posed for their parents—there was a careless beauty in their unconsciousness of becoming images in memory, just as there was a serious beauty in James's decision not to step in front of a camera. A few months later, I would be going to accompany James to his first day at college. Most children walked through an arch made of orange and black balloons, with the university's logo behind them, posing with cloudless smiles on their faces. James looked at the crowd and chose a side door to enter the building.

James did not give me permission to take a picture of him as a freshman, though he did allow me to take one picture of him at high school graduation, standing in front of an arch made of blue and white balloons. It was one of the few pictures I had of him after Vincent's death—before that they seemed to be always smiling and laughing and making faces for my phone camera. Perhaps it is not an exaggeration to say that James, before exiting the world, had begun to turn away, evading the cameras, evading attention, evading, even, the future.

When I dropped Vincent off near that high school on a September morning, we did not know that he was going farther than the school gate that day. When we sent James to college last September, we did not know that he, too, was going farther than the college campus. They both journeyed on more resolutely than I would have wanted them to, and they both crossed that great, awful distance after I said my last "I love you" to them.

XIII

Pebbles Are Not Boulders

I began to read the thirteen books of *The Elements* by Euclid a couple of weeks after James died. The week before that I read a book on mathematics for general readers, and I was quite taken by the statement that to excel in geometry, one has to have both intuition and logic. I was trained to be a mathematic prodigy when I was young, though I was not good enough to be a mathematician in the real sense, and geometry was my weakest subject in mathematics.

I wrote to my scientist friend Bonnie and told her that I was going to spend some time reacquainting myself with Euclidean geometry. I also told her that I did not yet know how our life would be lived but there was one thing I did know: do things that work.

"Do things that work" is a notion I have retained from Marsha Linehan's manual of dialectical behavior therapy, which I read a few times after my suicidal depression. There are other practical tips in that manual, some of which I've found helpful. For instance, holding a piece of ice in my hand is a quick and effective way to remind myself of the physicality of my body. Or, setting a timer if I need to worry about something beyond my control: I can rarely do five minutes of intense, focused, and unmitigated worrying—a mind wanders whether it's meditating or whether it's beset by anxiety.

But more than a decade after studying the manual, the most memorable thing for me is this notion: do things that work.

One could pressure that sentence a little more. Do things that work—for whom, or for what? After James's death, my friend Mona took care of our meals for months and checked in often to see if we were staying active physically. For a meal train she organized, many friends and colleagues—some coming all the way from New York— dropped off meals in front of our door. We were touched by people's thoughtfulness—a handwritten menu, an extra bag of treats for our dog, a card with an anecdote about James. None of these friends required a reply, or asked to see us in person. Do things that work—and I couldn't help thinking that all these friends, taking great care, were doing things that they knew would work for the mourners.

There is a gracefulness, when people know what it means to do things that work. A few days after James's death, my husband and I met Christiane for lunch, and later went to tea at Bonnie's house. Do things that work meant that we knew they were precisely the people who had the clarity to meet us where we were: they were not there to console us or to fix our problem; only, to spend a moment with us.

An old schoolmate of mine, who after Vincent's death told me that Vincent had been sent by god and had been taken away by god and my only salvation was with the church ("you think that is an option, but no, I think it's a necessity," she admonished me), asked to pay us a visit after James's death. I declined, not wanting to encounter her god again. I explained that it was not a good time, and yet she and another old schoolmate came and knocked on our door. The moment they sat down, my god-sent ex-friend gestured to the other friend and said, "Her children are in college now, and my child is in college too. So we are in a similar situation as you are. We don't get to see our children that often, either."

Did she suppose that I, grief-stricken, would be as witless as a four-year-old, accepting that make-believe logic?

Or did she mean that I should take their courageous selves as empty nesters as my model?

And yet now I think about it: those visitors would never have thought of themselves as outrageous. They installed themselves in our house for five hours, not leaving, not sensing that my husband and I were beyond exhausted by their presence. "Life is still surprising," my husband said afterward to Elizabeth, who was staying with us at the time. A few times she thought of telling the visitors they must leave, but that, she observed, would have embarrassed my husband.

There is a tragedy, and some people's social and religious conscience decrees that they must be present: to their minds they must be doing things that work. For whom, though? Sometimes people want to play a part in a tragedy that is, thankfully, not theirs personally: that, too, is doing things that work—for their own psychology.

"Do things that make sense to me," I've since then revised my goal from "do things that work." I could speak long monologues as Constance in *King John*, I could lament with loud keens as the mothers in Euripides's plays do, but those actions will not bring me any closer to James's mind, only, to his absences, so those actions do not make sense. Euclid, on the other hand, made sensible reading: James had a logical mind.

Do things that make sense—which, in the immediate

days after James's death, included studying geometry, reading a textbook on linguistic logic sent by Christiane, opening myself only to people who have the real strength and
understanding just to *be* in the starkness of my life with
me for a moment.

More important to myself, do things that make sense
means one must pressure one's thoughts and recognize
that some automatic thoughts are but pebbles.

The analogy of pebbles was given to me by Brigid when
she stayed with us the weekend after James's death. In a
moment of self-pity, I blurted out—"Am I not the worst
mother in the world?"—to which Brigid replied that we
both knew the answer to that question, and we also knew
the question was not a real question, only, a pebble of a
question. Better kick the pebble out of your way instead of
letting it stop you, she said.

If one is destined to live as a Sisyphus in an abyss, there
is good sense in distinguishing a meaningful boulder from
insignificant pebbles. A Sisyphus making a boulder out of
a pebble would only become a comedy. In the past few
months I've developed a habit of scrutinizing my mind: is
this thought a pebble of a thought, is this worry a pebble of
a worry, is this question, seemingly unanswerable, only a
pebble of a question?

Right after James's death, a thought, another pebble—
which didn't feel like a small pebble at the time—occurred

to me. I wrote to Deborah about what I called my "shy-ness," which was in truth a feeling of isolation. There were days when I thought that there would be no point writing from an abyss—from my abyss: people are largely outside it, and they won't be able to understand. "How does one write with this new knowledge, knowledge of a reality that's not likely to be understood by most people (and hopefully knowledge experienced by very few)?" I asked Deborah.

She replied that "there's no place for shyness in writ-ing," and quoted the last stanza of Wallace Stevens's "Tea at the Palaz of Hoon":

> I was the world in which I walked, and what I saw
> Or heard or felt came not but from myself;
> And there I found myself more truly and more
> strange.

The extraordinary nature of friendship with these clearheaded friends: they do not get distracted by my peb-bles of questions and thoughts, and they do not indulge me in pebble-mongering. A pebble is a pebble, which will not get more due than it deserves. If I aspire to live by intu-ition and logic, these are the friends who are more intui-tive than I am when intuition is needed, more logical than I am when my reasoning falls short.

XIV

Now and Then, Now and Now, Now and Later

In geometry, a point, according to the ancients' definitions, has no magnitude but has a position. Make that point a star or a mote, a giant or a bird nest, and there is no difference: it's only a point in the universe, which is indivisible according to Aristotle, and has no part according to Euclid. A point is an extremity.

Aristotle, in his effort to explain the concept of indivisibleness, compared a point in geometry to the *now* in time. So this *now* is as definite and concrete and yet as ineffable and incommunicable as a point in geometry. How long is *now*: a minute, an hour, six years, half a lifetime? How do you separate *now* from itself so that it is no longer *now*, but *now* and *then*, or *now* and *later*? *Now* is an extremity, too.

After Vincent died, I wrote in the book for him that, instead of now and then and later and much later, life without him was going to be now and now and now and forever. But I was not accurate in that sentence; I should have said *part of my life*. Because there was another part of that same life as a mother, which moved on from that point, in the most time-bound manner: bringing up James.

There were still days and nights, seasons and years, things to do, places to go. And, of course, there was the new reality of Vincent's absence—his physical absence, I should say. When the old framework for living was destroyed, a mother's job was to make a new framework.

Every spring I planted the seeds and waited for pots of herbs to grow, because James favored omelettes with fresh herbs. The homemade pancakes were still shaped to go beyond the letter Z—even if I could not meet James in that multilingual space where his mind kept himself company, I could still try, just as I could talk with Vincent from time to time, pointing out the first flush of roses, the cloudless September sky (September skies often take on the vivid blue it did the September day he died), the icicles above the garage door splintering the wintry sunlight, a new word I just learned from the dictionary.

(Or, a new confusion, in the case of the word "gorm-less." Vincent's favorite way to describe me was to say I was gormless, and sometimes I argued back, saying that no, I'd rather have the gorm, I am in fact gormful! It was years before I looked up the word "gorm"—which one would have expected to be the root word for the adjective "gormless"—but "gorm" means an undiscerning person, a fool; "gormless," wanting sense or discernment. How can this be possible, and where's the sense in this construction? When I first discovered this, I could feel myself throwing my hands up and asking Vincent to elucidate the situation for me. Or, suggesting that he could have done away with the adjective altogether. If the word "gorm" is sufficient, I would say, why "gormless"? Adjectives are my guilty plea-sure, he would reply, you gorm!)

(James, who used to like the word "gormless," too, stopped using it after Vincent's death.)

After Vincent died, the weekend breakfasts came with a cluster of lavender-colored chive flowers or a few mari-golds arranged on the edge of the plate, or a small jar of fresh roses on the table. In all those years of baking and knitting and choosing his own outfits, Vincent had a keen eye for beauty, so why not bring some touches of Vincent into a corner of our life; not to accentuate his absence, only, to acknowledge it. On St. Patrick's Day—mistakenly understood as Street Patrick's Day by James when he was three—there would be Irish soda bread at breakfast and a gentle reminder about the pinching leprechauns, as Vincent had always observed the tradition of wearing something green on the day. On James's birthday, on Vincent's birthday, and nearly every Saturday, I would bake a cake, a new tradition after Vincent's death. I used to buy cakes from bakeries, but it seemed to me good practice to honor Vincent, a very able baker, by baking for the family.

There were fencing practices to go to—James had had only two lessons when Vincent died, so fencing became a part of his life Vincent had not known. There were the long school years—middle school, high school—and then James outgrew Vincent. There were summer travels, and every year brought the same dilemma: should we go to places that Vincent had not been to, or revisit places Vincent had seen?

Inevitably both scenarios happened. We went to Sweden, Norway, Denmark, Finland, the Netherlands, Belgium, Switzerland, and Nova Scotia: the thought that Vincent had not seen what we saw was on my mind, perhaps on James's, too. And we revisited places that the children had loved in their years together. In Paris we walked past the playground where Vincent and James had climbed and spun, laughing wildly, and we stood near Notre Dame—burned down and still being rebuilt—and reminisced about the pigeons that had gathered on James's head and shoulders when he was three. In Edinburgh we stayed at the same flat in the Old Town because Vincent had loved the setting when we had stayed there, and our plan to climb to the top of Arthur's Seat gave way to other things, so I said we would come back next time, just as I had told Vincent the last time. In London the same old joke came back; it was while queuing in the Science Museum that James, aged six, invented the "most insulting insult" that made Vincent bend over with laughter: "Mommy, you're so dense that if we put you next to a black hole, you would not be sucked in by the black hole, but the black hole would be sucked into you."

Little did James know, and little did I know, that someday I would live with a black hole inside me, the precise shape of my two children.

Where do we go this summer? A few weeks ago my husband and I asked each other. There are places we could revisit, places we'd brought both children to: Japan, Spain, Germany, Italy, Ireland, Croatia. There is also the rest of the vast world that neither of them saw. But the discussion never went far. We'd always traveled as a family: it was our parental philosophy that we would spare nothing to bring the children to see the world.

What do you call parents who can no longer parent?

I stop myself from saying parents who no longer have

children. Death does not alter the fact that they are as much our children now as they were ten years ago. One of the very few things that surprised me, after Vincent died, was that he did not stay forever sixteen, as I mistakenly said he would, in the book I wrote for him. James grew, turning thirteen, fourteen, fifteen, sixteen, so Vincent did grow too.

And yet, only a few weeks before James died, feeling all of a sudden as though caught in a trance, I said to Elizabeth that somehow I felt stunted by life, and had never really moved away from when I was forty-four, when Vincent died.

The facts, however, remain as they are. I am fifty-one at the time of writing this book. And we are parents who can no longer parent. The noun form of the word is forever disconnected from its verb form. And it's the verbs, if one thinks about it, which tend to bear the brunt of death. Mothers are always mothers: some, now buried, can no longer mother their children; some, having lost their children, have no one to mother. (And some, mistaking "to give birth to" as "to mother," have never known the meaning of how to be a mother.)

Verbs can die, too, when children die. Dead verbs are like bees and ants and butterflies enfolded by the amber of time: to parent, to mother, to shape the pancakes beyond the letter Z.

The verb that does not die is "to be." Vincent was and is and will always be Vincent. James was and is and will always be James. We were and are and will always be their parents. There is no now and then, now and later; only now and now and now and now.

XV

Brothers and Best Friends

There was a time when I was not a mother. There was a time when I was not a writer—rather, a scientist. I became a mother before I became a writer—this thought has always been on my mind throughout my career. I am still a mother, only, I am different than most mothers. I am still a writer.

But James had come into the world with Vincent as his brother, who had become his closest friend. A child who loses his or her parents is called an orphan; a wife sometimes becomes a widow; a husband, a widower. But there are no such words made for those who have lost their siblings, or their best friends, or their children. Some losses are easily named, some remain uncategorized, uncategorizable.

James lost his brother and closest friend at twelve, and that loss was, is, and will always be beyond my fathom.

When Vincent was applying for a competitive middle school, he proudly wrote in his personal statement: "I know a lot about science because I've learned many things from my little brother." I savored that line because it captured both children, and I endorsed it, knowing that an admissions officer might conclude either that Vincent had a genius as a little brother or, more likely, that Vincent wasn't the smartest—at least, not the savviest—school applicant.

There was no way to explain that Vincent, who took pride and pleasure in his own brilliance, was only being truthful, and there was no way to explain that James was a child who, in second grade then, would be halfway through a meal and, putting down his fork, ponderously say, "Apparently the Higgs boson . . ." or, "Apparently the predatory tunicates . . ." Higgs boson? Predatory tunicates? All three of us marveled, not understanding how those topics entered family life at an hour when the world seemed mundane enough to be made of forks and spoons and chopsticks, not knowing, even, what those words, which we had barely or never heard of, meant.

Between the ages of five and twelve, James would

preface many of his sentences with the adverb "apparently," a habit that would vanish after he lost Vincent. Perhaps Vincent's death stopped the world from being apparent.

When James was six, I once asked him what was on his mind. (I often found him mysterious.) He explained patiently that what he saw would never be understood by me. "The world is made of dots and squiggly lines," he said, pointing one plump finger at the space around us. We were huddling in his bed, and there were books on the shelf, stuffed animals around the pillows, and posters of Pokémon on the wall: I could not see dots or squiggly lines. All I could do was to hug him closer.

Around the same time he also told me that he was "still" suffering from "monophobia." Monophobia? It was the first time I had heard the word, and I looked it up in a dictionary: a morbid dread of being alone. For how long had this little boy suffered from monophobia that at age six he would announce he was "still" afflicted?

I wished I had asked James then if Vincent could see and understand what my limited understanding had not allowed me to grasp. Was Vincent part of that world of dots and squiggly lines? I wished also I had asked James if Vincent helped alleviate his monophobia. But life would one day offer glimpses of answers to those questions.

Once, at a literary festival in Paris, I ran into Daniel

Tammet in the hotel lobby. He was talking to the late Australian poet Les Murray, so I did not have the opportunity to tell Tammet that his memoir, *Born on a Blue Day: Inside the Extraordinary Mind of an Autistic Savant*, was perhaps the only book, according to James himself, to have captured how he felt about the world. (The only time I remember James being a little impressed by me was when I told him that Daniel Tammet and I were at the same festival.)

Another book James read at the time—he was nine then—was *The Reason I Jump: The Inner Voice of a Thirteen-Year-Old Boy with Autism*, written by Naoki Higashida and translated by Keiko Yoshida and David Mitchell. James would point to a page and tell me that he too would do what Naoki did, and then he would turn a page and explain that here he differed from Naoki. In this case, I did tell David Mitchell how important the book had been to us.

Missing the opportunity to say something to Daniel Tammet, and being able to say something to David Mitchell—both were small in the scale of things and yet both would retain their meanings.

That a mother can do all things humanly possible for a child, and yet she can never understand the incommunicable vastness and strangeness of the world felt by that child; that a mother cannot make the world just a little more welcoming so the child feels less alone; that a mother cannot keep that child alive—these are facts I have to live with now, every single day, for the rest of my life.

For a time, in the six years and four months between the two children's deaths, I had some hope that we could raise James into adulthood, and that he would eventually find the right place in life. Surely we could figure out a way for the world to accept James as a person different than most people, maybe even for the world to benefit from his intelligence?

Those long hours from kindergarten to high school: one psychologist told us we were fortunate that James was compliant enough to go to school. We'd always known that James found school life boring, and yet we reasoned that it was good for him to be among children his age, to be part of the world even if he did not feel drawn to it. The alternatives of homeschooling or having him skip as many grades as possible, which were proposed by various people, were never considered by us. A schoolmate of mine, who had become an educational expert in Beijing, once confronted me because, she said, James should receive a tailor-made education, which should aim at making him into an Einstein. We were wasting his time and his talent, she admonished. I replied that we wanted James to have a normal childhood and grow up among other children.

But perhaps that woman had a point. Now that James

is on the opposite side of that border separating life from death, the decisions we made for him can hardly be defended effectively. If a child is not, in many ways, compatible with the world, should the parents gently usher him out of his cocoon—his room full of his books and toys, his parents and his brother, who loved him, and understood him more than the rest of the world could? Or should the parents fortify that cocoon to keep him safely there?

All those unanswerable questions, though there is one thing I know for certain: Vincent was the most important part of James's life. What security we had tried to build for James must have disintegrated when Vincent died.

I once worked on a children's book, *The Story of Gilgamesh*, and hired Vincent, who was in fourth grade, as a consultant. He read through the manuscript and asked a few questions, and later confessed that he was nearly in tears at the death of Enkidu, Gilgamesh's best friend, who was as close to him as a brother. A few years later, when James was in fourth grade, his Halloween project was to dress up as a character in a book. James read my book of Gilgamesh, and decided to be an antediluvian snake. We took him to a shop to pick up some green fabric that would make a good snakeskin, and he confessed in the car that the death of Enkidu made him "very, very sad."

The book was dedicated "to Vincent and James, brothers and best friends."

XVI

Now and Now and Now and Now

The thought occurred to me again, after James's death, that it's going to be now and now and now and now, every single day, for the rest of my life. This now is different than the now after Vincent's death. This now is about not the part but the whole of life. This now is more permanent, forever a beginning and always an end. This now, indivisible as a point, an extremity, is where we live.

And yet one has to find a way to live in that indivisibleness without being entirely separated from humanity. Is that even possible? Our life is pinned to that all-encompassing point of now, while the rest of the world, the one that is not made by my husband and me, is outside us, off the point.

In the immediate weeks after James's death, in so many conversations with Brigid, I tried to find the precise words for this new strangeness. And yet I could not articulate my senses. It was as though my life all of a sudden took on that quality of being made of "dots and squiggly lines," which could be understood by someone at James's level, but not at mine.

One Friday afternoon, Brigid said, "When Vincent died, you were outside time. That's why you could write that book for Vincent. You could meet him outside time, you could talk to him after his death. But I don't think you are outside time now."

No, I agreed. After James died, I was acutely conscious of the time line we shared with the world.

"But remember you talked about feeling lonely, even when you live in the same time with the rest of the world? That loneliness you talked about, I think, is because you're at a different place, a place outside space," Brigid said.

The place outside space, I now understand, is this extremity. It is this abyss. In this abyss I cannot really have the same conversation with James I once had with Vincent after his death. It takes radical acceptance, also, to know that I cannot do for James what I did for Vincent: Vincent was brought back to life by words, to myself, to his best friend, to the world that did not know him. I cannot bring James back to anything close to that.

"Should I set this book aside and write it later?" I asked Brigid once, feeling downtrodden in my inability to write for James.

Brigid said no. "You were here three months ago. You are still here. You'll always be here. The void that is James is not going to change."

The void that is James: before his death he had turned away. Or, perhaps a more accurate way to say this is that, in his life, he was forever turning away. Vincent, good at being in everyone's face, did not often allow James to absent himself entirely. What Vincent had done for James we parents were not able to do.

If I could ask James what prevents me from writing the book the way I could for Vincent, what would James say?

Most likely a single-word answer, "Oh," which might mean: Is that a surprise, or, I am not Vincent, or, Vincent helped you with that book but I won't, I would prefer not to.

Or he might also mean: But you must do something different. It's harder to write for me than to write for Vincent.

Yes, that I do know. After Vincent died, a parent of a friend of his wrote that she would always remember Vincent as the child who, in the street lit by an orange lamp, jumped higher, ran faster, and laughed more loudly than all the children around him.

She was talking about a night after a school dance, in the first year of high school, but she might also be talking about Vincent in his entire, short life. Vincent lived flamboyantly and demandingly. Vincent died because he did not feel that life could meet him: in poetry, in music, in beauty, in courage, and in perfection.

James was not Vincent. When James was in first grade, he explained that his best skill was not to be noticed by anyone. But wouldn't it be sad or lonely, not to be noticed by anyone, I thought. If the safest and the most comfortable place, for James, was a world where no one paid him any attention, was it a good place for him to be? Would he someday find that place less satisfactory?

A neuropsychologist who did a two-day assessment of James when he was in second grade explained to us that she had run out of tests for his mathematics and his logic. The only hope, she said, is that he will one day live among adults who are his intellectual peers. And who knows, she said, laughing a little, maybe he'll meet a chirpy girl who'll be his life partner!

She also showed us the results of one test, in which she'd asked James to draw a self-portrait in the rain. Look, she said, poor little boy! James in the rain wasn't under a tree, or under an umbrella. He didn't even have a hat on, she said. And the rain was not drizzle, or a light rain, or a shower, but a storm, a tempest! She talked about his anxiety and his loneliness, although how could we know about these; we could only approximate an understanding of James, not knowing him, not being him.

Still suffering from monophobia—no doubt James would have said that at eight, at ten. Surely that fear would have become part of life's permanency after Vincent died. Would he still have called it monophobia at thirteen or sixteen or nineteen? I now wish I had asked him.

A phobia would imply an alternative, in which the fear could be alleviated, or the situation inducing the fear could be avoided. A person suffering acrophobia would avoid heights, a person suffering agoraphobia would avoid crowds, but James existed in a space which he could not or would not share with another person, other than Vincent. Perhaps after Vincent died, James would no longer say he was suffering from monophobia. Perhaps the six years and four months, for him, was lived in a now and now and now and now, rather than now and then and later and much later. An extremity, an abyss, a situation that I, though loving him, could not change.

I had dreaded for six years and prepared myself for six years before Vincent's death. It occurred to me that during those six years when I was not preparing myself for James's death, he must have contemplated suicide, first, Vincent's, then at some point, as an option for himself.

XVII

Loneliness as a Pebble

After Vincent died, I asked a child psychologist, who was seeing James at the time, how we were to answer strangers' questions about our family's makeup. "How many children do you have?" someone asked me at a dinner after a reading, and someone else asked me while I was waiting for James at the fencing studio. When his two fencing friends, a brother and a sister, came over and saw Vincent's paintings around the house, the little girl, about to turn a decade old (as she told me with that specificity), blurted out in astonishment, "James has a brother?"

One does not want to lie about the most important things. Deaths do not change how we see ourselves. But one has to be realistic about the world, too. I've lived in two cultures—Chinese and American—and my experience is that people, even those with good intentions, tend to feel awkward around untimely deaths, suicide particularly.

I followed the psychologist's most helpful advice after Vincent died. "James lost his brother," I said to the two children when James, never quite verbal, went into a deeper silence. "But he may not be comfortable discussing it with you at the moment." And when their mother came to pick up the children, I took her aside and told her about Vincent's suicide, to which she replied with a natural grace, "I'm so sorry. That must be very difficult for all of you."

To the people who asked me how many children we had, I reproduced the psychologist's words verbatim: "We had two children, but lost one to suicide. I hope you understand that I'm not ready to discuss it." People tended to retreat to a respectful distance, nodding with understanding or confusion—who could tell. But once, while I was lying face down and half-naked on a massage table, the Ukrainian woman who was giving me the massage sighed deeply and said, "To think I only asked a simple question, but no question is that simple, right?"

The day before Mother's Day—eleven weeks after James's death—we went to a grocery store. The cashier, a young woman in her late teens or early twenties, asked me if I was going to do anything for Mother's Day. I smiled and shook my head, which seemed to disappoint her a little, so I asked about her plans. "I'm off in the morning, and I'm taking my mother out for Mother's Day brunch," she said proudly. I said how wonderful that sounded, and how lucky her mother was, which made the young woman—no, really, a kid, Vincent's or James's age—blush with happiness. "Do you have children?" she asked.

In that instant I knew that I could not always follow the protocol I had relied on all these years. I could hardly say to this young woman, her eager, friendly face still showing baby fat: I had two children, and I lost them both, so strictly speaking I don't have children, or more precisely, I'm a mother who no longer has children.

Instead, I shook my head, hoping that the ambiguity would end the conversation. She glanced at my hair. "Oh," she said with a little dejection, then gave me a kind smile. Perhaps my reply implied a pitiful situation: a woman her mother's age who either chose not to have children or could not have children, for whom Mother's Day would be just another day of the year.

Edgar's line came back to me at that moment: "And worse I may be yet: the worst is not so long as we can say, 'This is the worst.'"

The psychologist, who had taught me how to answer

the question about how many children I had, also told me an important thing when I had an interview with her before sending James to see her. "Never feel that you're obliged to show your pain to the world," she said. "Very few people deserve to see your tears."

I suspected she did not say that to James—she did not need to. James was a private person, but he was extremely private about his sorrow over Vincent. The only external sign: Vincent, flamboyantly handsome, used to wear his hair long, and in the six years and four months since Vincent died, James had not once cut his hair. James, who resisted drawing any attention to himself, was the boy with the longest hair in middle school, in high school, and in his short half year at college.

At Vincent's memorial I read two poems, one by Elizabeth Bishop, one by Marianne Moore. The Bishop poem, "Argument," spoke of my thoughts as Vincent's mother. "Days that cannot bring you near / or will not..." The Moore poem, "Silence," was read on behalf of James (though it would speak to the essence of our whole family): "The deepest feeling always shows itself in silence; / not in silence, but restraint."

Vincent would have disagreed with that line. He lived at a spectacular height, unrestrained in his joy and in his despair.

After James died, there was a moment—a week—when

I said to three different people that I felt lonely. Both my therapist and Brigid noted the importance of that statement: up until then loneliness had not been a noticeable emotion in my life. In fact, the feeling of loneliness—though expected, though inevitable—had taken me by surprise. My characters are lonely. James was lonely. Vincent was lonely, too, despite having many friends. But I myself have rarely felt lonely.

Deborah wrote me after I told her about my loneliness:

I think that everyone around you right now wants to help you. In order to help, they have to think about what would be helpful to them if they were in your situation. For almost everyone (at least, in their projections), the emotional reaction would come first—an overwhelming, explosive outburst of grief, hair-tearing, self-recriminations—and would be followed by more rational, intellectual reflection much later, once that tempest had blown over. So for you to go directly to the intellectual side of yourself confuses people; so few people are capable of going directly there that they don't believe you can; they feel you must be ignoring or repressing the reaction that they are sure they would have. It also means that they can't offer the help that they would want to receive in your place: they can't wipe your tears, hold you while you wail; it pushes them out of the room, in a way. Hence the loneliness of mourning as you do: not only are you mourning but the form of your grief and your ways of approaching it are not understood, or are misinterpreted.

I was amazed by Deborah's articulation of the situation. Then the feeling of extreme loneliness passed.

To philosophize is lonely, but to philosophize is also to learn to walk past some emotions, including that momentary loneliness, and say: these are but pebbles that should not and will not stop me.

XVIII

Marking Time

In March, my piano teacher lost her eighty-five-year-old father. He had been taking an acting class, and on the last day of class, he invited his wife to his final performance in New York City. Afterward, they took a stroll in the city, and he collapsed. A few weeks later, I resumed my Wednesday piano lesson, and I made a bouquet of tulips and daffodils and hyacinths, all white, from my garden. I was particularly fond of the double daffodil called the Bridal Crown, the petals creamy white, with a soft yellow in the center that reminds me of Irish butter.

I walked across the parking lot and paused a couple of times, inhaling the sweet scent of the bouquet. Two men, coming out of a church, complimented the flowers. I thanked them and one of them said, "Hey, aren't they for me?"

"The flowers are for a dead man," I snapped and walked on. People, by behaving predictably and unimaginatively, are good only at confirming what I already know, and I think to myself: where you are is where the husks of life gather; where you are is where I won't be. There is little comfort in that knowledge, but still it is a relief that death has made it easier for me to pay no attention to the husks of life.

Cristina, the piano teacher, was indignant when I told her about the men. It was a consolation that some emotions could remain clear in a life muddled by deaths. I asked her about her father's life and about his funeral, I asked her about her mother's mourning, her own exhaustion, and the many loose ends death leaves behind. She then said, "How could you come to a piano lesson right after your child died? I would have stayed in bed forever."

She was talking about the lesson that took place on the Wednesday after James's death. I had known it was important not to cancel the piano lesson. When I met Cristina at the studio, she was holding a little jar of flowers—it was still early in the year, cold, wintry February. We sat in front of the piano for a moment and agreed that there was nothing—absolutely nothing—we could say, so we began the drill. (I'm a beginner. I had started to take lessons with her three months earlier.)

How could you come to a piano lesson right after your child died? I don't remember what answer I gave Cristina, but it doesn't matter. The only answer, to many similar questions, is the same: What else can I do but to go on with the things I *can* do, to keep my body nourished and active and my mind occupied and sharp?

The friends who took turns to stay with us in the weeks after James's death were all subjected to my piano practice. In fact, I wouldn't call it proper practice. My skills were rudimentary, but even the beginner's waltzes and minuets in a piano book for children felt too much at that time: I could not summon any energy to meet the music's moods.

Instead, most of the time I plink-plonked the only thing that did not make any musical or emotional demands on me: I played the drills from Hanon's *The Virtuoso Pianist in Sixty Exercises*, a series of exercises Cristina's Italian piano master called "demented."

In those days I repeated the exercises like an automaton. There's really very little musicality, my husband said at one point, comparing the demented exercises to the book of Russian music and the book of Bartók exercises I had played earlier. And when my friend Elizabeth visited, we would read quietly before I went to play the piano.

Then she could no longer read because Hanon would make thinking impossible. The only thing she did while I was practicing was to send emails about academic bureaucracies.

And yet in those days I was obsessed with the Hanon exercises. (I am still obsessed with them.) I played first the regular way, then I played them with one hand staccato and one hand legato (and switching), then one hand pianissimo and one hand fortissimo (and switching), then adding a variety of rhythms while mumbling to myself: "California watermelon" or "watermelon California" or "sugarplum" or "raspberry."

I can play these exercises only with my eyes closed. If I open my eyes, my fingers, strange objects that don't always look quite connected to my brain, trip on the keyboard, forget the patterns, and land on the wrong notes.

Half an hour, sometimes forty or fifty minutes pass. Then I open my eyes. Vincent and James are still smiling at me from the pictures on top of the piano, and the few objects next to the pictures—a spelling bee trophy of Vincent's, a deer antler we had picked up on a hike near our old house in Oakland, a pebble that must have had some meaning when it was first found on the beach in Monterey Bay—remain their unchanged selves. In this indivisible *now* the objects still retain their *then*.

And my life is here, in this *now*, still baffling. Outside my *now* are people: friends who sustain me, but also strangers. These strangers can be unthinkingly oblivious or unthinkably cruel. Some of them want my attention and some revel in my tragedy, but in an odd way, they sustain me too: one wants to know the best of people, but one also wants to know the worst of people, which is not a necessity for living, but it is a necessity for writing fiction.

"Gods are stubborn. So am I," Herakles says after having been tricked into killing his own children by Madness, whose father is Heaven and whose mother is Night.

Life is stubborn. So am I. I have conceded to make this abyss my habitat, every single day, for the rest of my life. But I shall live in this abyss only on my terms.

I suppose many people, looking at my life, ask some variation of the question, aloud or to themselves: How did this happen?

Every single day, as I pause in the middle of typing, or cooking, or reading, or practicing on the piano, or as I pause on the stairs, going up, going down, I can hear myself say: How did this happen? How can this be possible? How did I end up in this extremity called my life? It is a fact that these questions, unanswerable, fill in the gaps between two moments. They are not pebbles. They are not temporary. They make up that boulder that I cannot carry out of my abyss; my only way, so far as I can see, is to coexist with this boulder, in this abyss. Two hands, barely touching or with fingers intertwined, what difference does it make?

The second book in Elizabeth Jane Howard's the Cazalet Chronicles is titled *Marking Time*. I find myself thinking of that phrase often. The phrase "to mark time" is defined in the *OED* this way: "Originally *Military*, to march on the spot, without moving forward; (*figurative*) to act routinely, to go through the motions, esp. while awaiting an opportunity for something."

Where can we live but in days?

And the days after James's death are but an abyss.

How does one live in an abyss?

By marking time, how else does one live?

Music is about marking time—perhaps one day I will play Chopin's nocturnes, perhaps not. "Ten years?" I said once, "I'm giving myself ten years. What do you think? Will I be able to play his nocturnes then?"

Cristina, a professional who made an exception to take me on as a student ("Most adult students are hobbyists," she explained to me the first time we met), looked at me thoughtfully and said, "Yes, that's possible."

Then, ignorantly, I added, "And in five years I will play Chopin's études."

Cristina looked at me sternly and said, "Now you're being very funny. That you cannot do, not in five years, not in ten years."

In music you can't skip a passage and pick up somewhere else—although you can, of course, when you practice. But life is neither practice nor rehearsal. The absoluteness of life—whether it's life in an abyss or not—is that in each day, time has to be marked before the next day arrives.

Playing the Hanon exercises is a way of marking time, and so are all my other activities: working through Euclid's geometry books; going to piano lessons; taking a midday walk with my husband (in cold February rain, in a fragrant April breeze, in an unrelenting June heat); reading, writing, baking soda bread or yogurt coffee cake; pruning and feeding the roses, planting new seedlings, going outside to yell at the newborn bunnies that are feasting on my garden and then giving up when the bunnies cannot be stopped; weeding, weeding, weeding and then one day giving up because weeds are part of nature, too, and things in nature merely grow.

Anything that keeps a body moving and a mind focused on the immediate present is marking time. After Vincent's death I spent weeks knitting up the stock of yarns he had bought. I also found a couple of mindless games, which he had downloaded on my phone, and for the past six and a half years I have been using his log-in name, 57oss, and playing the games before bedtime.

Anything that marks time falls into the realm of the living. The dead, not going anywhere, do not need to mark time. They don't necessarily help us mark time, either.

XIX

Abyss, Again

The first time I used the word "abyss" to describe my life was when I was in a psychiatric ward in New York, where I stayed for three weeks after a suicide attempt in 2012. Life after a major crisis stands preternaturally still, the way I imagine the windless calm in the eye of a hurricane—this I would one day learn from Vincent's death, and learn again from James's death, but the first time that stillness beset me was in that New York hospital. My mind was distant from my body; both were distant from that essence which I would call my self.

The day after my arrival, when my brain was less foggy, I went to the nursing station and asked for a pen and a student's exercise book. Sometimes I put a single word on a page. Or a combination of words. Or a line of a poem from ancient China—I had memorized hundreds of poems when I was growing up, an activity that I had known by instinct would set me apart from people around me. In the hospital the pen and the notebook were my habitat, as those volumes of ancient poetry had been for me when I was ten, twelve, fifteen. A habitat is not always a place of security, but it offers a possible hiding spot. There is no guarantee of safety; only, a better chance at eluding the predators.

Then my friend Tom came to visit, and he brought with him *War and Peace*, *Anna Karenina*, and an essay collection by Montaigne. My mind became less agitated, and I felt less estranged from myself: those books, made of words not mine but known to me for years, became a refuge.

Words, words, words. Words form castles on the solid ground and in the clouds, words become armors and prison walls, words make riptides and quicksands. One can never take words for granted; one cannot always trust words; and yet, where else can my mind live but in words?

A few hours after my appearance in the ward, a middle-aged woman peeked in through the half-open door of my room. (No door on a psychiatric ward is closed during the day, or locked at night.) "I washed my hands before I went to get this for you," the woman said, and held out a pair of disposable underpants, folded as though it was a precious gift.

I did not know if I should decline. She put the offering into my hands and then sat down on a chair to talk about herself. There was nothing wrong with her, she wanted me to understand, just as she could see there was nothing wrong with me. Circumstances, however, made it necessary that she must stay in the hospital. "People in Washington, DC, are after me," she said. "That's why I'm hiding out here."

"Oh," I said.

"Don't you worry. I have people in Washington who are watching out for me, too," she said, winking at me.

Around me, from morning to night, was the sometimes symphonic but more often disharmonious orchestration of thirty women who all lived in various degrees of despair. When freedom was lost, when sanity was lost, and when reality was lost, words became one of the few possessions that could not be taken away. No one's life was entirely private. Everyone had a story, and many of the women were eager to tell their stories to me, which, instead of broadcasting some special qualities about me, reflected, I suppose, the desperate need for everyone to speak and the lack of anyone willing to listen—this, certainly, is not a phenomenon specific to a psychiatric ward. In civilian settings outside the hospital, I've often found myself to be the recipient of people's life stories.

"Get thee to the nuttery," a cartoonist friend jokingly messaged me the other day. Isn't the world the most inclusive nuttery? Very few people are like Bartleby or my children; very few people will say: I would prefer not to.

Perhaps everyone I met in that ward deserved a novel; I knew I was not the one to write them. "Life is a tragedy for those who feel, a comedy for those who think," said a mind from the past (credited variously as Horace Walpole, Jean Racine, Jean de La Bruyère). Going by that saying, nearly every person in that ward was living in a tragedy: feelings, reliable or unreliable, were abundant among the inmates. I say nearly everyone because I did not count myself among them: thinking, rather than feeling, was what led me into that world behind a metal door with a sign that warned: ELOPEMENT RISK.

Earlier that year, when I tried to wean myself from an antidepressant, my mind slipped into unreality, which was made of thought and logic, only thought and logic that I now know—and perhaps knew even then—could not be trusted. "Brain chemistry manifested as a cognitive crisis," a doctor explained in the hospital. "We are all bags of chemicals," my friend Elizabeth said recently.

And yet I could not untangle myself from that unreality. Every Saturday, after James's piano lesson and Vincent's tennis lesson, we had lunch at a quaint place called Caffe Trieste in Berkeley, sitting in the sunny breeze, chatting about nonsensical things. I remember watching Vincent savor the lava cake, which was a favorite for us all; I remember relishing James's joy when he cut the giant meatball in half. I remember talking and laughing with the children, going over the grocery list with my husband, and sometimes turning to the TV on top of the counter, which was often tuned in to European football matches. I remember also feeling coldly detached from myself, from the world around me, including my children.

For months the shell that was me continued to live, taking care of my family, teaching, writing, going out on book tours, reporting to jury duty, taking our new puppy to training classes, but my thinking self was outside that shell, watching with indifference. Which of them was me, which was my twin; the twin who I had once been told existed in the room next door but whom I had never seen? Which was the real me: the one who had always striven to be wise and kind and calm, or the one who felt a profound indifference to all those efforts?

If my children cannot stop me from slipping into unreality—I thought then, looking at the boys, who at ten and seven seemed to be living in a moment of great hilarity, with endless jokes and laughter—if this will not save me, nothing will.

And nothing did. Six months later, I was in that psychiatric ward. Once I opened the books Tom had brought me, the world of chaos retreated. There is no real salvation from one's own life; books, however, offer the approximation of it. When I began to write in the student's exercise book again, my words became more coherent, less entrapping. Writing, too, offers the approximation of salvation.

An old woman, who had spent most of her days conversing with her dead family members, asked me once what I was writing in my exercise book, and I showed her the word "abyss" on a new page. She squinted at the word for a long moment and sighed. "Abyss, abysmal, abysmally," she said. "I feel abysmal, yes, I feel abysmal. Do you feel abysmal? Abyss, abysmal, abysmally."

I too felt abysmal, and it was in that moment I realized that abyss, like bliss, is hard to communicate to another person. No one's abyss is more or less abysmal than another person's, just as no one's bliss is more or less blissful than another person's.

The old woman wore a pair of ruby-red shoes that she had picked up from donations to the patients. The shoes did not fit, and she would break into tears because her feet hurt, or her body ached, or the medications froze her brain, or her sister would not come back to answer her questions—among the dead people she argued with, the one she argued most often with was her sister, a fact I gathered from sitting next to her and listening to her monologue.

A young woman had fashioned a piece of black-and-white plaid tablecloth around her paper gown as a miniskirt. She always asked politely if she could tag along when I was taking a walk. It took thirty steps to walk from one end of the hallway to the other, and in the days before I started reading I walked and counted my steps until I reached ten thousand.

The young woman was from Bosnia, and during the Kosovo War, her mother, who was from Kosovo, had walked out on the family and returned to her home village. The young woman was twelve then; and since her mother left she had not seen or heard from her mother again.

Day after day she waited for me to put down my books so she could walk with me. She talked about her mother and the summer days in Bosnia, she talked about her older siblings, who were scattered around the world, and she talked about her ambition to become an actress one day. At one point she paused and assessed my outfit. I was wearing a T-shirt Tom had brought, which had Tom's book cover printed on it: an extraordinarily beautiful woman with a lost look in her eyes. The young woman studied the T-shirt and shook her head. "Once you leave here, you must buy some white shirts of the best quality, a very smart jacket, and roll your sleeves just to here." She pointed to a position on her own skinny arm. Then she squinted at my glasses. "Yes, those are good frames, but when you leave here you should get new ones. You should only wear Prada."

Memories of her mother, aspirations and plans for the future, the miniskirt—none of them solved the young woman's problems in that present moment. "I'm not mad," she said to me. "I got my heart broken by a man. But now they're not letting me leave."

I am not mad—Constance says that when she mourns the young Arthur, and every woman in that ward said that, too. And yet every single woman there was in an abyss. What is the difference between being mad and being in an abyss?

In the hallway I was not the only compulsive walker. A petite woman in her sixties, who wore a pink Chanel jacket and a matching skirt, walked away most of her time, too— very slowly, as she had an arm and a shoulder in a sling, and I could see the walking caused her physical pain. I did not know what kind of pain she suffered beyond that broken shoulder; she was the only woman who did not seek a conversation with anyone, and when she was approached by others, she had little advice to dole out.

We nodded at each other when we crossed paths, many times a day, but we rarely talked. Sometimes her adult daughter came to visit her, and sometimes her ex-husband, an old man in round spectacles, came. Once a young colleague was there. Whoever came to visit would walk the hallway with her, not talking much.

Had the woman in the pink Chanel suit decided to tell me her story, I would have listened to every single word, though perhaps my respect for her was the same as hers for me: we all live in stories that cannot be fully told; very few people in the world deserve our tears.

When Tom came to visit for a second time, he spoke about his own sojourn in a New York City psychiatric hospital not too long before. "There I turned the corner, and guess who was coming down the hallway? Joan Didion. Well, I thought to myself, if she hasn't figured out about life, who else among us stands a chance?"

I recently reread *The Year of Magical Thinking*—and calculated. Tom encountered Didion a few years after the publication of that transcendent book. Writing, offering a transient refuge, is an approximation of salvation, nothing more. Who among us stands a chance facing an abyss?

And who among the writers I've loved has summoned up the abyss in the precise way that I've experienced it? There is no shared abyss; we each dwell alone in our own.

XX

A Life Worth Living. A Livable Life

My friend Katherine came to visit in early June, and asked how much I thought James's suicide was connected to Vincent's. No doubt this was a question on the minds of many who knew our situation. "Do you think," Katherine said, "that Vincent's suicide might have given James a sense of possibility?"

We were rowing in a twin kayak then, past clusters of box turtles gathering on the half-immersed fallen trees of the last season, past a lone heron watching its own shadow and then swiftly breaking the water's surface, resurfacing with a fish in its mouth. How extraordinary, I realized then, when a friend, not dreading discomfort or unease, has the courage to ask the most difficult questions. Despite catastrophes, I am still myself—this, I've learned, is not necessarily obvious or even graspable to some friends; not all of them treat me as the intellectual equal of my old self.

When Katherine asked about the connection between the two children's suicides, I felt immensely grateful. The natural questions to follow—though she did not ask—are: How did my suicide attempts affect Vincent? Did I, by trying to end my life, also make him see that as a possibility to end his own suffering? Was I the person to have pointed at what separates life from death and said, Look, that partition is not as solid as people make it out to be?

"Whether life is or is not worth living amounts to answering the fundamental question of philosophy" is Camus's statement. Had someone asked me, when I was deep in my suicidal depression, if life was worth living, I would have replied, yes, of course. I was a mother, and life was worth living, if not for myself, then for my children. My then therapist asked me if I was afraid of losing my children, and I said that my fear was for them, not for myself. I was afraid that they would lose me, and my fear on their behalf made me my fiercest enemy.

People sometimes say of those who've attempted suicide or succeeded that they are selfish, or feebleminded, or attention seeking. People feel hurt, are offended and angry, perhaps out of fear or incomprehension, or perhaps because for once they cannot claim the center of someone else's story: suicide is among the most absolute and exclusive actions in life. (My mother said to me about my attempt: "Why did you do that to me?")

Those who've attempted suicide or succeeded in suicide are not necessarily eager to kill themselves; rather, the pain can be such that nothing short of wiping out their physical existence can end their suffering. People don't call those with cancer or other illnesses selfish or feebleminded or attention seeking, but in my experience, people tend to be harsh and critical of those who suffer from suicidal depression or other mental illnesses. Is it a sense of superiority that makes people insensitive, or, more precisely, a deep sense of fear—where you are is where I don't want to be, so I had better condemn you first to ensure my safety.

That extremity of mental pain was what I experienced when I felt suicidal, and I suspected this was close to how Vincent felt. Though I don't think this was how James felt.

A few weeks ago, I asked Deborah and Brigid about the late writer John L'Heureux, who, afflicted with Parkinson's, chose assisted suicide at the age of eighty-four. Deborah and Brigid had both worked with L'Heureux the weekend before his death on some final edits, and I remembered talking with both of them about the experience of working with someone who was in a composed, even cheerful, mood about that coming Monday, when he was set to die. This time, when I asked about him again, in connection to James's suicide, they both said that they did not think of L'Heureux's death as suicide. "It was a release from difficulty—it was undergone with the perfect knowledge that there was nothing good ahead that wouldn't be tainted by illness and that others would be forced to spend their own last days caring for him if he didn't take action," Deborah wrote. And Brigid said that she could see why someone might call his death a suicide, but to her it was not.

And yet I could not help but feel that James's thinking might have been close to L'Heureux's. The difference was that James's decision was not made in old age or with an incurable disease threatening a rapid decline.

Life, in an absolute sense, is worth living, just as art is worth pursuing, science is worth exploring, justice is worth seeking. However, the fact that something is worth doing doesn't always mean a person is endowed with the capacity to do it, or that a person, once endowed with that capacity, can retain it. The gap between worth doing and being able to do is where aspiration dwells for the young and decline lies in wait for the old.

Is life worth living? Had I asked Vincent, I trust that he would have said yes, but then he would have pressed me with his variations of the question: Is this life, which may be worth living, worth suffering for? If life is worth suffering for, should there be a limit, or should one have to suffer unquestioningly, all in the name of living?

Is life worth living? Had I asked James, he would have declined to answer. I would prefer not to say, he would have replied, in which one could sense the seed of negation.

A few years ago, when I met a psychiatrist, he asked me about that unreality I slipped into in 2012, and I said, a little shyly, that everything, in the end, came to that central question—is life livable? And my answer, after months of struggling, had been no. The psychiatrist nodded and then told me an old story from Norse mythology. In the wild darkness there is a long hall, brightly lit, warm, with windows open at both ends. A bird flies in from the window at one end and in a moment dashes out of the window at the other end. That hall, the doctor said, is life, and we're all birds coming out of the cold darkness for a moment and then returning to the cold darkness the next moment. "My advice," he said, "is that you never ask that question again. Is life livable? We don't really have the time to form a thorough and thoughtful answer."

Is life livable? Had I asked Vincent, he would have pointed out that he had given me the answer by choosing suicide. Had I asked James the same question, I suspect he would have said yes. James would've called life "perfectly livable" just as he called the mediocre cafeteria food "perfectly eatable."

Vincent lived through his feelings, deep, intense, and overwhelming feelings, and he died from his feelings: a life worth living, in the end, did not prove livable; an acutely artistic and sensitive soul might not always have the means to prevail in this world.

James thought hard: deeply, philosophically, and privately. He died from thinking: a livable life might not be worth the trouble; a livable life, he must have concluded, was not what he wanted.

My intuitions as a mother were such that I understood Vincent's feelings and foresaw the dire outcome of those feelings, and yet I could not alleviate his pain enough to keep him alive. But with James I was even more limited: I could only reach for his mind without grasping it. My intuitions about James were put into words only once—to James, a few weeks before his death, in fact.

Why? I will never be able to answer that question.

On the last day of his winter break, I had a conversation with James, telling him that by my calculation only ten percent of life is made of things and people we love, and for that ten percent—the real joy of living—we must endure the other ninety percent. I told him that I myself had not had enough understanding of this statistic, so I couldn't have told Vincent this when he was alive. "But remember, Vincent was a perfectionist," I said. "So even if I had told him that, that ninety percent of life would have been difficult for him."

James nodded.

I then said that my hope was that his temperament—which was calm, dispassionate, self-effacing—combined with his strong intellectual grasp of science, language, philosophy, and logic, would mean that life would remain livable for him. "Always think of that ten percent," I said to him. In that same conversation I also pointed out to James that his stoicism and his resilience would be things to rely on in life, with which he agreed, not verbally, but with his gentle smile.

But I was wrong. A livable life might not have been attractive or engaging enough for James. A livable life fell short at some point. Stoicism could mean that death, like life, could be endured. James died as a result of thinking, not feeling, just as in my own case it was thinking, rather than feeling, that had led me to the border between life and death. One could say that James thought himself into a corner; one could also say that James thought himself out of his loneliness, which was not only about losing Vincent, though losing Vincent must have been the saddest thing that happened in James's life. His intelligence would have worked better for him had he wanted something more from life. But in a few conversations we had around the time he went to college, he confirmed my fear that he was not interested in anything external or worldly. Wealth or fame would not allure him. Self-expression would not interest him. Knowledge—language, philosophy, history—would give him pleasure, but that pleasure would remain private; he saw little need to communicate it to another person. It was not often that he would find an incentive to speak: if he did not understand something, he could not possibly speak; if he understood something thoroughly, there was no point in speaking.

"Rarely is suicide committed (yet the hypothesis is not excluded) through reflection," Camus wrote in *The Myth of Sisyphus*. The line stood out to me when I reread the book after James's death. I cannot be certain enough to say he did exactly that, and yet his suicide did have an element of calm inevitability, the result of long and thorough reflection.

James died on Friday, after his last class that week—Japanese, in the early afternoon. He walked out of life as though that was the natural conclusion to the week. He walked farther than anyone did on that day, but not, I think, farther than Vincent. I am not the kind of person to believe in an afterlife where the brothers would reunite, but I am certain that James, walking across campus on that day, would have looked at the world where there was no Vincent, and thought that it was a place he could and would leave behind.

But of course my thinking is but conjecture. Every single psychologist and psychiatrist will tell me that no one ever knows what really happens when someone chooses suicide.

There is a Japanese shop in downtown Princeton where we sometimes went with James. When we went to pack up his things from his dorm the day after he died, I noticed in the trash can an empty sushi box from the shop, so I knew he had gone there to get his favorite sushi for one of his last meals. Before Brigid went back to New York, I asked my husband to go to the shop with her to buy a few of our favorite Japanese snacks for her to bring home. There was no reason for Brigid to need anything from that shop, but there was every reason for us to be able to step into that shop again.

I went there a few days later by myself. For one second I thought I might have gone blind or that I might faint, but experience has taught me that in this life of extremities one cannot rely on one's feelings entirely. Another customer squeezing past me would see only an ordinary woman, contemplating two different brands of miso, and it would be by thinking rather than by feeling that I would return myself to the form of that ordinary woman, whose only concern was to choose the right miso.

One can be dazed by the strangeness of life and by the insolubleness called here and now, but one has to remember that all these things are natural when one lives in an abyss. One does not keen like the mothers in Greek tragedy, one does not tear one's hair like Constance, one does not bang the walls that are not there, one does not raise one's voice because the voice, once raised, speaks not of one's thinking mind, but of a primitive pain that does not leave any space for thinking. Like James, I prefer to live by thinking.

Why would a woman who knew suffering give birth to her children? That question from Vincent—I never had a good answer for him. I advocated for patience, and for the possibility of change—I myself had just returned from the bleakest time of my life, I had in my teenage years come close a few times to suicide, so I understood him, I said, but things might change, and sometimes they might change for the better.

"But do you really believe that things *will* get better?" Vincent pressed me once. We were sitting in his bed then. He was a thirteen-year-old who looked all of a sudden very young. The transparent pain on his face reminded me of a much younger Vincent, of the summer before kindergarten. His best friend, Mari, had told him that she might not marry him because she wanted to marry her brother. Vincent returned home in a daze and stayed immobile in bed for hours. What kind of five-year-old feels so acutely the pain that belongs to someone older?

After a few hours, Vincent sat up and ripped out an

empty music sheet from his piano book. "O LOVE, O LOVE, O HEARTLESS LOVE," he wrote in block letters. "THROUGH YOUR HEART. FOR YOUR LIFE."

Mari's mother was in awe and begged for a photocopy of the page. I was in awe, too, but I was also alarmed. I despaired, really. I wished then—and I still wish now—that Vincent had not been born with the capacity to feel what he felt in life. But "wish" is such a weak, useless word.

But do you really believe that things *will* get better? That I did not lie blatantly and offer Vincent blank and vain promises—in retrospect this gives me some solace. I said I could never say things would get better for sure, but that his feelings might change, and he might think differently at a later time. He sighed, and agreed to "give life another chance."

In the end, there are only a limited number of times that one can give something or someone another chance.

Had Vincent lived, had he asked me the question now, I would have answered differently. I know suffering, and I have written well about suffering, but I also know that one's relationship with one's suffering can change. For Vincent, I don't think life would ever have become easier. However, I do believe that we learn to suffer better. We become more discerning in our suffering: there are things that are worth suffering for, and then there is the rest—minor suffering and inessential pain—that is but pebbles, which can be ignored or kicked aside. We also become less rigid: suffering suffuses one's being; one no longer resists.

I wish I had shared these thoughts with Vincent when he was younger. It might have helped him a little, or it might not have changed the course of his life or my life. But wishes are but artificial flowers. I did not know back then that one could learn to suffer better. I did not even know it after Vincent's death. I learned this only after James's death.

I do not know if these thoughts would have helped James at all. For years, he had perfected suffering as a state of being, and in the end, he too turned away.

XXI

Minor Comedies—for James

Children die, and parents live, but it doesn't mean they go on living like Humpty Dumpty or pathogens of infectious diseases. When Vincent died, some friendly people faded out of my life. "I don't want to intrude on her" and "I don't want to make her sadder by talking about Vincent with her" were, I was made to understand, how some people felt. As though any one of them could outshoot life to injure me; as though anything they said would make me sadder!

A father with whom I communicate once a year—he lost a fifteen-year-old son to suicide—told me that when, after a few years, some neighbors finally approached him

and said something kind about his son, he found it meaningful. A neighbor of mine, after James died, saw me in
our driveway, scooped up her little dog, and waved and
scurried away. No doubt things felt difficult for that father's neighbors in Boston, or for our neighbors. True
compassion takes courage.

A few days after James died, a friend of my husband's
came from California to spend some time with us. A law-
yer by profession and a dispassionate man by nature, he did
not feel it necessary to sugarcoat life for us. (He also came
to visit right after Vincent died, and was the first person to
have raised the question whether James might consider
suicide.)

When I told him that I sensed that our situation had
spooked some people, he nodded. "Yes, I can tell you
that there is general unease among people who know you,"
he said, referring to our friends and acquaintances in
California.

People sometimes feel awkward or apprehensive
around grieving parents, particularly if the children died
from suicide, perhaps infinitely so when a family lost two
children to suicide. I wish people had the honesty and
courage to say, I'm not capable of handling this difficult
situation, or, I'm uncomfortable because I don't know
what to say, rather than telling themselves that they are

absenting themselves out of respect for the bereaved parents.

The notes and letters coming in after both my children's deaths: the most comforting ones were those that expressed shock, confusion, helplessness, and the pain of not having the right words. All those feelings were close to ours. I cannot think of a more consoling connection I felt after both boys' deaths, than when I read those notes. Words may fall short, but they cast long shadows that sometimes can reach the unspeakable.

Inevitably there were people who wrote that they *understood* our pain because, though they hadn't lost a child or they didn't have children, they had lost a parent or a beloved pet. Kindhearted and well-intentioned people: don't make those comparisons. These messages are not compassionate; they are clueless, even egotistic. It's all right not to understand the situation—neither do the parents! And it's more than all right to acknowledge that you cannot find the right words—I, a professional who has worked with words for twenty years, can't either. It's not quite all right when you make yourself the center of the message: no need to remember your own losses, and no need to provide advice about how to overcome grief from your own triumphant experience.

After James's death, an overeager local news outlet

rushed to publish a breaking news report about James, connecting his suicide to Vincent's suicide and my past suicidal depression. ("Alas, not the kind of journalism that will win them a Pulitzer Prize," a colleague said, though the reporter did reach out to me, asking me for a comment.) The news, picked up and amplified by the Chinese media, somehow made my personal life the center of an orgy. ("Your own Kate Middleton moment," my friend Gish, who was in Shanghai then, wrote, referring to the malignancy in the Chinese media.)

Vincent would have been hurt, even enraged, by what I will write in the following paragraphs, but James, I suspect, would have been amused. He had a higher tolerance for people's cluelessness, and in that respect James and I are similar.

That my private life could move strangers to rush in to express either sympathy or malice is not unexpected, but sometimes dark comedy arises precisely because what's expected happens as predictably as one suspects it will.

A childhood friend, agonized by what she read in the Chinese media, wrote to me and said, baffled: "You're not explaining yourself." Explaining, wherefore?

To people who have written to offer your prayers, your goodwill, and the sorrow you have felt on my behalf: allow me to thank you here.

But strangers, more so than friends, sometimes have

unrealistic expectations. People wrote to offer friendship, leaving their phone numbers for me to call, some venturing to tell me that their friendship was what I needed at this difficult time. To those who have written with your numbers and your wish to talk to me on the phone about my life: it was kind of you to offer, but friendship takes years to cultivate, and deep, mutual understanding, and a bereaved mother's priority is not to start a friendship from scratch. (My husband, as logical as James was, did point out that such offers also reflected the fact that I am a public figure. No doubt there are people in worse situations than I, who don't get these zealous offers from strangers.)

To the father who wrote with the proposal to drive your daughter to my house so she could play beautiful music on her violin: it was nice of you to come up with the idea; it was also unintelligible to me that you dedicated most of your long message to your daughter's musical and academic achievements. I am a bereaved mother who happens to teach at an Ivy League university; I don't work for the admissions office.

For the writer I haven't met: it was flattering that you wrote and said you wanted to dedicate a book to me (I would have declined); but it was not quite right you would then send the whole manuscript to me, and it was beyond comprehension that you went on to ask me if I could help you find a publisher.

For an acquaintance of whom I once thought fondly: it wasn't quite all right to send your colleague's manuscript to me so that it could, in your words, provide me with a useful distraction from grief; and it went a little beyond the pale that it so happened that your colleague also needed to find a publisher, and you had offered up my help, despite the death of my child.

For the stranger who wrote to say your life was more tragic than mine, who asked me to call you—"at your earliest convenience"—so that you could tell me your story as an inspiration for my writing: I'm sorry to hear that you have experienced tragedies in your life, and I'm afraid that I won't make the call.

And for those kindhearted people who were keen to offer silver linings on religious, spiritual, and other grounds: I'm afraid I must disappoint you. Sometimes there is no silver lining in life. Some consolations are strictly and purely for the consolers themselves. Please hold on to your silver linings, as I must decline.

Grief cheapened by cliché, by wishful thinking, and by self-centeredness of various kinds—this is another reason I never use the words "grief" or "grieving" when I think about my children. "Grief" is a word used often in those emails sent to me.

We like to set our hearts on a finish line, hoping to take the right actions so that we can reach that finish line fast and with the least hassle or pain. Perhaps this urge reflects a desire to mark time in a different way: to harness time for gain. And yet in life, time cannot be harnessed.

Marking time after a child's death is not about overcoming grief or coming out of a dark tunnel—all those bad words sound to me as though bereaved parents are expected to put in a period of hard mental work and then clap their hands and say, I'm no longer heartbroken for my dead child, and I'm one of you normal people again, so now we can go on living as though nothing had happened and you don't have to feel awkward around me.

I am not a grieving mother. I am the mother who will live, every single day, for the rest of my life, with the pain of losing Vincent and James, and with the memory of bringing them up.

To the Chinese media who ran the headlines about the deaths of my children coupled with my decision to abandon my mother tongue or my turning my back on my mother country ("a traitor deserves to be punished" was a message conveyed without subtlety, sometimes explicitly); to the giddy tabloids who called me the murderer and the killer of my children; to the trolls who fabricated sensational stories about my life (apparently, I often abandoned my children for a glittering high society in Europe); to the Alex Joneses of Chinese origin who hypothesized that I belonged to a cult to lure young people (including my own children) into suicide and proposed that the university I teach at should investigate the cases of students who died by suicide in the past few years and their connections to me; to the psychological experts who did public psychoanalysis on me; to the astrologists who looked at my birth information for a postmortem of my fate; to the gossipmongers and hobbyist commentators: I am sorry for whatever losses you have suffered or whatever deficiencies you were born with that make you, unavoidably, who you are and what you are.

I've known people—in China and in America—who treasure their malevolence, and who revel in the pain they inflict on others. Whether they do this out of profound unhappiness or a profound delusion of power (or both) I do not know; what I do know is that they cannot be helped, and they cannot help themselves.

Some years ago, a middle school classmate of mine committed suicide in Beijing in his thirties. In our younger years he and I were close. He was sensitive, fragile, proud, and lonely—but how else could a boy of artistic and soulful temperament be? Ask Chopin, ask Rimbaud, ask Vincent.

My friend was good at painting, I was a budding accordionist, and we loved and excelled in poetry equally. He became a designer, and shortly before his death, he wrote to me and congratulated me because, in his words, I had prevailed in being a dreamer.

After his death, our old schoolmates, as a collective group, seemed to have very little sympathy. Rather, there were jokes and there was gossip, as if a young man's death, especially an artistic and sensitive young man's death, deserved nothing more than laughter and mockery. I remember feeling relief on my friend's behalf, rather than pain and loss: the world is a cruel place; why stay here among these cruel people, people who will never dare to go to where you've found your freedom?

When the Chinese media were having a giddy time with my life, Brigid told me several times not to read the news, but I explained that a writer must know the world as it is. Nothing coming from China surprised me—how could those strangers do anything to surprise me, when I am my mother's daughter?

Life is a comedy for those who think. I have always believed that thinking, rather than feeling, will stand me in better stead. The only time this comedy became less reliably comic was after Vincent's death. A woman whose daughter was a friend of Vincent's came to visit, and told me that her daughter had not received a farewell text from Vincent, as two other girls had. Her daughter had always considered Vincent one of her best friends, the woman said, but Vincent had not treated her daughter as a real confidante, which was not fair.

It was December, and the woman had asked me to go

out to the garden to tell me this because my husband was in the kitchen. I remember the snow on the ground, deep that winter; I remember the chill in the leaden air; and I remember feeling that I would go blind and faint, just as later I would feel momentarily overwhelmed in the Japanese shop. I could not, in that moment, get myself out of that deep abyss I was thrown into by another person.

I must have said something polite to the woman—it didn't matter what, because she was there to file a complaint about my dead son, and she was expecting me to say all the things I could and then she would likely conclude that I failed to appease her. If she decided to forgive me or Vincent, she would congratulate herself on her magnanimity.

I remember coming back into the house in utter confusion; confusion I have rarely felt—not even at the news of my children's deaths. I did not know if I should tell my husband what the woman had just said to me. Vincent had sent a farewell message to me minutes before he died, but I had not known, until then, that he had said farewell to two friends.

This information is a fact now, among many facts of my life.

But before a fact becomes a mere fact, it has all the power to derail a mind. I hesitated, but only for a moment—I could not withhold this important information from my husband. I asked him to sit down and then I told him what the woman had just said to me. My husband looked ghostly pale, stricken like a parent in a Euripides play. When he could speak again, he said, with a great and agonizing restraint, that it felt as though Vincent had died a second time.

Children die, and parents go on living in an abyss, but that, I now know, is not the worst thing. Beyond that abyss is yet another abyss, and one has to rely on one's thinking to stay in the more meaningful abyss. People can hurt only our feelings, not our thinking—not unless we let go of the independence of our minds.

And people who intentionally or unintentionally hurt other people: I have come to the conclusion that they cannot help themselves, and they cannot be helped. This is only an acknowledgment, and it is not understanding or forgiveness, neither of which I will give.

XXII

Things I Never Told My Children

When we were growing up, my mother dictated that my sister and I must serve as her targets anytime she felt angry. And she seemed to be full of unpredictable rage in those years; any little thing could lead to an explosion. I once got beaten after I received high scores on a school exam, and the reason she supplied for this beating was that I looked too smug for her liking when I reported the news. I once left a scarf at the school gym on a winter day; already frightened, I unwisely and preemptively offered the solution that I would get up early the next morning and go to the school gym to retrieve the scarf: the next thing I knew I was lying in large basin of water. I was eight then, and the basin was one of those old-style metal ones, a meter wide, which every family used for doing laundry before washing machines became more widely available in the mid-1980s. My mother had kicked me hard, and I had tripped and fallen backward into the basin. I remember being waterlogged like a turtle with its belly up, not being able to get myself out of the basin right away, and my sister, frightened, pale, hovering over me, not daring to offer a hand because my mother was still raging and cursing.

And yet I am my mother's favored daughter, and she claims to have loved only me. My sister has her own stories, some I remember, others I won't know unless she tells me. After our father died, she told me that when she was six, she dropped a jar of laundry detergent on the floor by accident, and our mother slapped her so hard that afterward, she studied herself in the mirror, certain that her face, so swollen and deformed, would never straighten itself again.

I've noticed that every time my sister or I tell a story about being beaten by our mother, inevitably we giggle, as though we were embarrassed by our memories, or else we were talking about something that was slightly distasteful but also very, very funny.

People do laugh from the abyss. A few years ago, a nanny in New York killed two of the three children in the family. The children's mother, when she was put on the witness stand at the trial, was reported to have "laughed

nervously as she tried to maintain her composure." I suppose that nervous laughter was out of the need to detach
herself from the most horrendous memory. I sometimes
mention that detail to my students, because their characters often behave predictably, crying or screaming in pain.
Deep pain doesn't necessarily make a character scream, I
explain. Look at that mother, she laughed! My students
are often dumbfounded: They are still young, but it is my
job to tell them that sometimes poetic words about grief
and grieving are only husks. It's their good fortune that
they haven't learned that sometimes people don't have the
luxury to wallow in clichés.

Worse than the beatings we received from our mother
were her piercing words. I, more than my sister perhaps,
protested about how we were treated. My mother would
then enter a different kind of rage, calling me a murderer,
accusing me of intentionally making her angry so as to
drive her mad, so as to drive her into an early grave.

Whether she beat me or not, her rages would end with
her telling me that I would die an ugly death.

My mother has always maintained that she never mis-
treated us. "You write fiction for a living, you make up stories, and you tell lies," she said a few times. The last time
she said that to me was shortly before my suicide attempt.
My parents were visiting us in California. Two days before

their flight, my then therapist begged me to stop them from coming. But that wouldn't do, I explained to him. He then said, despairingly, "She's going to kill you."

My mother did not kill me. I tried to kill myself. And the very last thought on my mind was seemingly logical: if I'm losing my grip on this real life and slipping into unreality, I would prefer that my children do not have to deal with a mother gone mad.

A question my mother liked to ask us when we were young: do you want a dead mother or a mad mother? According to her, a mad mother would be better than a dead mother. I was never asked what I thought. What would a mad mother do to me? Beat me, berate me, tell me that I was responsible for her bad mood and, especially, that I was responsible for robbing her of her youth. All because of you, she would scream at me, because I had to give birth to you I'm now growing old. Even at seven I knew her logic was horrendously flawed.

What would a dead mother do? Certainly not prophesy that I would be her murderer.

When I was a teenager, I was told repeatedly by my father that because my mother loved only me, it was my responsibility to maintain the peace in the family by keeping her happy. I remember on a particularly difficult day—my sister and I were both teenagers then—my sister said to me in a dark despair: "She's gone mad. I think she's gone mad for real this time. Remember, she's your responsibility. You have to keep her alive and happy."

Nobody knew that I had always thought a dead mother would be better than a mad mother. That thought, too, was on my mind when I felt too bleak to live: it's not my children's job to keep me alive; in fact, it's my job to protect them from myself, if I cannot save my sanity.

I have shared very little about my past with my children—I did not want to be one of those mothers who feel compelled to take center stage in their children's lives. I once visited James's second-grade class for a social studies project, and told the children that what I most hated when I was a child was candy. The kids gasped, incredulous. I didn't explain that I hated candy because adults in my childhood always thought they were doing me a favor by giving me a piece of candy. I could never say: I would prefer not to. If I clasped the candy in my hand without eating it, there was bound to be an adult who would take the candy out of my hand, unwrap it, and thrust it into my mouth—I always spat it out later when no one was around.

James came home and told me that I was a legend among the second graders. "Did you know Mommy hated candy as a child?" he asked Vincent, who gasped, too.

Do I now regret it that my distaste for candy might be among the very few things my children knew about my past? I don't know. And in the large scale of things, whether I regret it or not doesn't matter.

Though one thought did occur to me after Vincent's death, and again after James's death. The same thought has also occurred to my husband. We each grew up with a difficult parent: he's a much, much better father than his father; I, a much, much better mother than my mother.

Children of abusive parents might grow into rebels, or they might become escape artists. I have never been an overt rebel, but I have honed my craft as an escape artist all my life. "That need only children of abusive parents know," I said to my husband. "The need to keep one thing to yourself and making sure no one can take it away from you. You have it, I have it, but our children didn't have it. If they had had that, they might not have chosen suicide."

"But how much more they'd have suffered," my husband said. "And we didn't want them to suffer."

"No," I agreed.

And yet they still suffered. Only, not under tyrannical parents. We had spun them cocoons and fortified them. And in the end, our endeavors did not keep our children alive. They became escape artists, too.

XXIII

Children Die, and Parents Go on Living

At the beginning of the summer I returned to the university swimming pool. The semester was over. The students were gone. James would have finished his first year in college. Vincent would have graduated from college this year.

I am the slowest swimmer in the pool. The second slowest swimmer is a man who looks at least ninety years old. An older Japanese woman once told me, after I got out of the water, that more than once she had sat on the bench and watched me swim. The reason, she explained with sincerity, was that she had never really learned to swim properly—she simply knew how to swim from her childhood. Most swimmers in that pool are such good swimmers, she said, she can't quite study their form because they are too fast; but I can watch your movements, she said, and she had been trying to imitate my strokes. I laughed, and told her I had just learned to swim. I am the slowest swimmer in the pool, and I swim in slow motion because I have to think with every stroke and every kick.

For most of my life I was extremely afraid of water. When Vincent and James were small boys, I thought I should be able to get into a pool with them, so I hired a student from the college I was teaching at then, and when that student graduated, I hired another. My progress through the lessons, on and off for more than a year, was steady enough that I could get into the shallow end of the pool with the boys. Then they learned swimming themselves. Then they were old enough not to need me in the water with them.

After Vincent died, I thought I would tackle swimming again, this time for myself. I hired a student lifeguard, who was patient; she told me that her mother couldn't swim, either. Sometimes I asked the student about this or that movement, and she would have to swim herself, trying to figure out which part of the body and what muscles to focus on to achieve the desired effect.

Those who have learned swimming in their childhood

tend to swim unthinkingly. For some people, the same must be true in life; for them living is a natural process. This has never been the case for me or for my children.

I now go to the pool at six thirty in the morning, and I am still the slowest swimmer. Swimming was something I learned for my children's sake; it's something I do for myself now. I count between breaths, I kick my legs, I stretch my arms, calculating the angle at which my hands enter the water, I turn my head—all these movements, all action verbs, require some conscious thinking.

Sooner or later, however, my mind drifts elsewhere. In the water it is now and now and now and forever now. My life, strange to others, is stranger to myself, but that doesn't really matter. In this strange life I can still think—think about things and then scrutinize those thoughts; think through things and then start all over, accepting that, short of one's death, all finalities in life are provisional.

I think about how to make the next stroke less feeble, about the chapter of the novel I shall be writing after swimming, about the Chopin nocturnes too sophisticated for me to play, and about the oriental poppies that I loved when I was a young girl, which I have been unwilling to plant in my garden. The Chinese name of the flower, Beauty Yu, is an homage to a famous courtesan who killed herself for her lover, a general who was to face the first emperor of the Han dynasty in his final and fatal battle the following day. (Perhaps next year I shall plant some oriental poppies, along with the rose named Sweet Juliet.)

I think about Lear's howl and Cordelia's stubbornness. I think about Richard II's hollow crown and the tears of his queen, with which she curses the gardener because he has brought the news of her husband's downfall. I think about our upcoming trip to Wales to meet my friend Cressida—two days after James died, Brigid asked me if there was one thing I wanted that could be made to happen, and I said that I wanted to go to Wales in the summer—we'd talked for some years about going there and hearing James speak Welsh to people.

I think about counting days and marking time, and my thoughts, inevitably, return to my children. That a mother can no longer mother her children won't change the fact that her thoughts are mostly a mother's thoughts.

I think about Vincent's clothes, which I had packed and then unpacked to hang up in the closet after we moved into the house: bright T-shirts, light-colored pants, at least a dozen woolen and cashmere scarves, which he had chosen for himself in Scotland the summer before he died (while laughing at his vanity). After James died, I took a fleece jacket from Vincent's closet, of a cool, grayish blue, and started to wear it even though it was a little small for me. (It was the first time an object that used to belong to Vincent had become mine.)

I think about James's clothes, too, jeans that are of the same brand and the same three dark shades, T-shirts with mathematical illustrations, twenty pairs of identical socks—plain white, unlike Vincent's socks, all in bright colors. When we brought James's belongings back from his dorm, Brigid laundered all the clothes and folded and packed them in a suitcase. For months I have been walking into his bedroom, thinking that I should return the clothes to the closet and his underpants and socks to the chest of drawers; I cannot do it. The only thing I did was to pick up some loose clothes hangers and hang them in his closet, free of any clothes. All the same it is some small measure of order I have brought to this life of extremity.

James's retainers are in a box on his desk. Vincent's retainers are in a box on his shelf. A few weeks after James's death, his dentist's office sent a reminder about a routine checkup and cleaning. The dentist has seen James since we moved to Princeton; before that, I had always brought the two children to their dental appointments together in Berkeley. The dentist in Princeton, a tall and bearlike man, was extremely gentle with James for the next six years, and I had to reply to the text sent from his office, saying we would not be able to make it to the appointment because James had died.

A few years earlier, a student of Christiane's died from suicide, and she wrote to me:

These are sad days for me; a student I was close to for the past four years died last week. I will speak at his service in the Chapel tomorrow and want to share here with you this line from a German poem that I intend to read (my informal translation):

There are times in life when the world seems to stand still, and when it turns again, nothing is as before.

If the world *seemed* to stand still once, it *is* stiller now.

That a mother can do all things humanly possible for her children and yet cannot keep them alive—this is a fact that eschews any adjective.

Children die, and parents go on living—this, too, is a fact that defies all adjectives.

When Vincent's phone was returned to us, only a corner of it was fractured. When James's backpack was returned to us, among a stack of papers, all unused, there was a pencil. It was broken into halves at the same moment James died. These are facts, too. And I think about them often.

In this abyss that I call my life, facts, with their logic, meaning, and weight, are what I hold on to. It's not much, this holding on, and yet it's the best I can do.

And this book for James—I don't think it will live up to his standard. There was never a single argument between James and me, as there were many arguments between

Vincent and me. Vincent had made demands I could not meet in his life, but James put up with what I was not able to do for him. Within my capacity I have loved and taken care of James. Within his capacity he allowed me to mother him.

Sometimes a mother and a child are like two hands placed next to each other: only just touching, or else with fingers intertwined. Then the world turns, and one hand is left, holding on to everything and nothing that is called now and now and now and now.

A Note About the Author

Yiyun Li is the author of several works of fiction—*Wednesday's Child*; *The Book of Goose*; *Must I Go*; *Where Reasons End*; *Kinder Than Solitude*; *Gold Boy, Emerald Girl*; *The Vagrants*; and *A Thousand Years of Good Prayers*—and the memoir *Dear Friend, from My Life I Write to You in Your Life*. She is the recipient of many awards, including a PEN/Faulkner Award, a PEN/Malamud Award, a PEN/Hemingway Award, a PEN/Jean Stein Book Award, a MacArthur Fellowship, and a Windham-Campbell Prize, and she has been a finalist for the Pulitzer Prize. Her work has appeared in *The New Yorker*, *A Public Space*, *The Best American Short Stories*, and *The PEN/O. Henry Prize Stories*, among other publications. She teaches at Princeton University and lives in Princeton, New Jersey.